A New History of the Picts

STUART McHARDY

Luath Press Limited

EDINBURGH

www.luath.co.uk

First published 2010
This edition 2011
Reprinted 2012
Reprinted 2014

ISBN: 978-1-906817-70-1

The publisher acknowledges subsidy from

Scottish
Arts Council

towards the publication of this book.

The paper used in this book is recyclable.
It is made from low-chlorine pulps produced in a low-energy,
low-emissions manner from renewable forests.

Printed and bound by
CPI Group (UK) Ltd, Croydon, CR0 4YY

Map by Jim Lewis

Cover images: Man and horse from a rubbing of the Martin Stone
by Marianna Lines; stag image from the Grantown Stone.

Typeset in 10.5pt Sabon by
3btype.com

STUART MCHARDY is a writer, musician, folklorist, storyteller and poet, and has lectured on many aspects of Scottish history and culture both in Scotland and abroad. Combining the roles of scholar and performer gives McHardy an unusually clear insight into tradition. As happy singing old ballads as analysing ancient legends, he has held such posts as Director of the Scots Language Resource Centre and President of the Pictish Arts Society. McHardy is a prolific author, and has had several books published, including *Tales of the Picts*, *Tales of Edinburgh Castle*, *The Quest for the Nine Maidens*, *On the Trail of Scotland's Myths and Legends* and *Edinburgh and Leith Pub Guide*. McHardy lives in Edinburgh with his wife Sandra.

Dull Stone

Digitally enhanced image from photograph by Noble.

Acknowledgements

While all the ideas in this book are mine I would like to thank a variety of people for their assistance in bringing this book to print. My friends in the Pictish Arts Society have, over many years, through the course of often vigorous debate, helped to clarify my own thinking and in particular I would like to thank Sheila Hainey, Marianna Lines and Molly Rorke. Likewise many of my students over the years have helped me see things clearer, most notably Tim Walkingshaw. Dr Dauvit Broun of Glasgow University was kind enough to let me see a pre-publication version of his 2008 paper in the Bibliography, and Dr Brian Moffat of the Soutra Trust was extremely helpful in matters concerning the 'miracle food', the Kale Pea. My editor Alice Jacobs was a delight to work with and my son Roderick was of great assistance in amending the text. Thanks are as ever due to my wife Sandra for her continual support and encouragement. Finally thanks go to Gavin MacDougall of Luath Press for his continued support for Scottish culture at all levels and to all the staff of Luath; Leila, Senga, Anne, John-Paul, Christine and Jo, who worked hard to make it all happen.

Contents

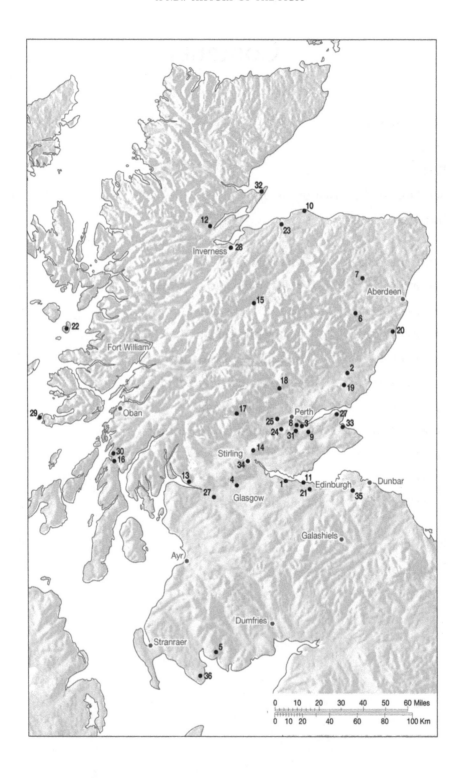

Map locations

1	Abercorn	site of short-lived seventh century Northumbrian bishopric.
2	Aberlemno	location of significant symbol stones.
3	Abernethy	possible Pictish capital and early Christian site.
4	Antonine Wall	Roman wall across Central Scotland
5	Anwoth	furthest south example of Pictish symbols.
6	Balbridie	Third Millennium BCE timbered hall.
7	Bennachie	significant mountain with ancient monuments.
8	Carpow	Roman site on the Tay near Abernethy.
9	Collessie	location of carved stone with warrior.
10	Covesea	cave with symbols and First Millennium links to Europe.
11	Cramond	Roman villa.
12	Dingwall	Highland town.
13	Dumbarton	capital of Strathclyde Britons.
14	Dumyat	fort of the Maetae.
15	Dunachton	possible site of battle in 685CE against Northumbrians.
16	Dunadd	capital of Dalriada.
17	Dundurn	Dalriadan fort.
18	Dunkeld	important Pictish religious centre from early ninth century.
19	Dunnichen	possible site of battle in 685CE against Northumbrians.
20	Dunnottar	major fortified site.
21	Edinburgh	capital of the Gododdin, Dun Etain.
22	Eigg	site of martyrdom of St Donann.
23	Forres	site of death of king Dub.
24	Forteviot	ancient prehistoric site important into ninth century at least.
25	Gask Ridge	possible site of Roman's first attempt at frontier.
26	Govan	important early Christian site in Strathclyde.
27	Inverdovat	site of death of king Constantine c.877
28	Inverness	capital of Bridei mac Maelchon visited by St Columba.
29	Iona	home of the Columban church.
30	Kilmartin Glen	pre-Christian sacred site for millennia.
31	Moncrieffe Hill	possible site of battle c.728.
32	Portmahomack	site of recently excavated Pictish monastery.
33	St Andrews	important early Christian site.
34	Stirling	strategic hilltop site at the centre of Scotland.
35	Traprain Law	possible capital of the Votadini, later the Gododdin.
36	Whithorn	important early Christian site, St Ninian.

Preface

> Since the Union (of 1707) the writing of the history of Britain has been a more or less political process, the viewpoint of the historian depending on the individual's position on the meaning and consequences of the Union and on the process of securing the creation of 'North Britain' and 'South Britain'... A small country sharing a small island with a world power will never have a quiet life (as Pierre Trudeau described Canada's relationship with the USA as 'being in bed with an elephant').
>
> [Barclay 2002]

THE RESULT OF THE process described by Barclay has been that much of Scottish history is effectively Anglocentric. The needs of the British state to have a cohesive past have over-ridden much of the reality of Scottish history. This process has been well described in the remarkable *The Very Bastards of Creation* by James D Young, in which he looks at Scottish Radicalism in the period from 1707 to the close of the 20th century. As the recent work by Doron Zimmerman [2003] has shown, there is still a great deal to be understood about even as recent a Scottish historical phenomenon as Jacobitism. The dominant thrust of Scottish history writing has been to stress the similarities between Scotland and England by downgrading the differences.

England was part of the Roman Empire for 400 years – the idea that Scotland was ever anything other than outside the frontier is risible. Because of this, tribalism in England was on the decline from the beginning of the First Millennium while it survived in Scotland till the 18th century. England was subjected to successful invasion by Danes and Normans, and while Scotland lost vast tracts of its territory to Scandinavian invaders, the area from Edinburgh to Inverness, Argyll to Aberdeen was never conquered. It is perhaps a truism to say that most of Scotland's history during the period from *c.*1000CE to the Union of the Crowns in 1603 was dominated by the need to resist invasion from England but it is none the less relevant to who we are in historical terms. Ethnically of course, now that we can see the bias of 18th century ideas more clearly, we can see that all of the British populations are mongrels – the idea of pure ethnicity is as intellectually pathetic as it is politically vile. Unfortunately ideas still abound that the 'Celts' are a separate ethnic group but thanks to the seminal works of Simon James [1999] and Brian Sykes [2006] this idea can now be understood for the romantic idiocy that it is. By showing that the very idea of Celticism developed from a need to resist Britishness, James has helped to create a clearer understanding of the past few centuries. While it is generally accepted that the Picts spoke a Celtic language, as did the Scots, and that the Vikings were Germanic speakers, they are all our ancestors. Language is important in helping us to understand the culture of different peoples in the past, and the relationships between them, but can tell us nothing about ethnicity.

Scotland at the dawn of history

SCOTLAND FIRST APPEARS IN written history when the Romans marched north to fight the tribes they called Caledonians. This name appears to be virtually synonymous with Pict. The Romans had already subjugated what is now England, which was to remain a part of the Roman Empire for almost 400 years. After the supposed great Roman victory of Mons Graupius – we only have the Roman side of the story – *c.*80CE, there are no further mentions of staged battles but Roman sources do mention heavy casualties in the north. The ongoing attempts to subjugate what is now Scotland saw the Romans fail time and again to conquer the Picts. In the period after the Romans left at the beginning of the fifth century CE the situation in the north of Britain changed dramatically. As the Anglian kingdom of Northumbria began to expand from its base in the north-east of England in the sixth and seventh centuries, the tribal peoples to the north came under considerable political and military pressure. By the time that we have more written history to call on, from the sixth century onwards, the earlier tribal peoples of Scotland seem to have merged into four main groupings, most of which were still essentially tribal.

These were the Picts north and east of the Forth–Clyde line, the Scots in Argyll, the Britons of Strathclyde whose territory stretched from the Clyde to Carlisle, and, in the south-east the Gododdin, whom the Romans had previously called the Votadini. All of these groups of people except the Scots appear to have been predominantly P-Celtic speaking. That is, they spoke a form of Celtic language which can be seen as a precursor of modern Welsh and Breton. This accounts for the fact that the oldest known Welsh poem, *Y Gododdin*, was written in Edinburgh at the dawn of the seventh century.

The Scots spoke a related Q-Celtic tongue which developed into modern Scottish Gaelic, which is itself related to modern Irish. After managing to halt the expansion of Northumbrian power in the seventh century the Picts began a process of consolidation which saw them eventually allying with their cousins the Scots in the 10th century to form the united kingdom of Alba, which in time became known as Scotland. From the eighth century onwards much of the Hebrides and northern Scotland fell under the control of the Vikings and eventually became subject to the

Kings of Norway. Over the next couple of centuries the south-west and south-east of Scotland were drawn into the new kingdom and in the Middle Ages the islands and the north were ceded to the kings of Scots to create what we nowadays think of as Scotland. Today, Scotland is to a great extent the lands north of Hadrian's Wall which the Romans never did manage to conquer.

Introduction

THE TITLE OF THIS work is *A New History of the Picts*, but any attempt at a truly definitive history of the Picts is, at the moment, impossible. The Picts were the people who were in what is now Scotland when the Romans arrived from England in the first century, a people who while being non-literate left behind a wonderful corpus of carved stone monuments which continue to inspire and puzzle people today. They had no cities, or even towns according to the Romans, and appear to have been an essentially tribal, pastoral society. Perhaps in the future, as a result of increased archaeological investigation we may have a more complete picture. The problem we face at the moment regarding archaeology is that until recently very few of our resources have been devoted to investigating our Pictish past. Due primarily to the effects of being locked in a political Union with a larger neighbour, and the consequent Imperial need to develop a 'British' history, in which the Romans played an important part, much of our scarce resources have been devoted to digging up Roman remains. While the Romans are of importance to our understanding of Scotland's past, these archaeological investigations are of extremely limited use in understanding the development of indigenous societies. The limited written Roman sources that have survived do tell us a considerable amount about Scotland and its inhabitants in their time, but their actual influence over the development of Scottish history has been, and continues to be, overstated.

The essentially English-based focus in the development of this British history has given rise to the situation where one can go into the magnificent new Museum of Scotland and find a considerable concentrated display of Roman artefacts while references to the Picts are scattered thinly throughout the Early Peoples section of the museum. In part this is because the nature of the brief Roman occupation of parts of southern Scotland left us so much more in the way of recognisable artefacts than the indigenous tribes of the period who were living in scattered and self-sufficient communities. The simple reality is that we have not excavated as many indigenous sites from the Pictish period as we have of the Romans. To deny the importance of the Romans to our understanding of Scotland's past would be an exercise in futility, but the fact that so many of our resources have been devoted to investigating their temporary presence here tells us a lot more about the inclinations of our own historians when looking at Scotland's history, than it does about the realities of Scotland's past.

Archaeology is conservative by its very nature, and increasingly the tendency is to leave things alone till better methodologies of understanding arise. This attitude is understandable given some of the destruction wrought in the early days of archaeology and the significant levels of investigation that can now be carried on through recently developed techniques such as aerial photography, geophysics, and soil analysis. However there is another, and entirely understandable, limitation on archaeological investigation. To try and understand any archaeology one must have a series of questions that can be asked of the artefacts, structures and landscape variations that are encountered. In this sense the investigation of Roman outposts, signal stations and other sites are straightforward in that so much is known about them that a series of very specific questions can be postulated. For instance the types of nails used by the Romans in wooden buildings changed over time, and particular types can give specific dates of occupation. Other technical aspects of Roman fort construction, coinage and weaponry can similarly be given relatively precise dates. Recently there has been a growth in the excavation of Pictish sites and following the same requirement for a clear set of questions to be asked, they have in the main been early Christian sites. Again this is because we have a great deal of comparative material from elsewhere, as well as a considerable amount of documentation about religious, and economic practice in such institutions. To investigate a pre-Christian Pictish site is more difficult, in that to date there have not been so many clear questions that could be posited. Partly this is because so few of them have in fact been investigated but there is another limitation. Little attempt has been made in our institutions, constrained by the limitations of an essentially Christian and 'Britishist' historical approach, to understand what preceded Christianity in Scotland. The use of the term pagan, like Celtic, is something I will try to avoid as both words have been bandied about in so many different situations, often by people meaning totally different things, as to render their meanings indeterminate. I believe that there is much that can be understood about the beliefs and perhaps even practices of pre-Christian sacral behaviour and will look at this extensively in a forthcoming work on early Pictish symbol stones, but to describe such behaviour as pagan is not particularly helpful. Even the idea of a cohesive single religion, akin to the big world religions that exist today suggests a conformity and uniformity that is highly unlikely to have existed before the monks arrived.

Because we have no written records from the Picts themselves they can seem almost historically invisible. Scotland as a whole has virtually no surviving documents from the First Millennium and what has survived, is in later copies of supposedly earlier works. It seems clear that after the arrival of the Christian monks, particularly Columba in the 560s, the Picts must at the least have known of writing, but nothing that we can claim to be Pictish has survived. Our limited knowledge is based on such sources as the Irish Annals, the King Lists of the Picts that survived in Continental monasteries, and early historical works, none of which are indigenous to Scotland, never mind Pictland. So we know of the deaths of kings and of major battles and other general information which made its way into the annotations of early Annals [see below p.89]. Even the King Lists are problematic in that no son ever succeeds his father [see below p.113]. Whether this is due to some form of succession through mother-right is still being debated but it does tell us that the Picts do not seem to conform to easily understood historical models. The situation is complicated by the existence of the Pictish symbol stones, one of the most under-appreciated collections of art in human history. While clearly in existence before the arrival of the Christian monks, the tradition of carving symbols on stone soon itself became Christianised and led to the development of many truly wondrous sculptured monuments. Even the function of these stones is unclear and discussion continues as to the possible meaning of the early symbols, many of which were adopted and used in later, obviously Christian, sculptures. What we can be sure of is that in the First Millennium in what we now call Scotland there was a people who in time were seen as quite distinct from the other peoples of the period, the Scots of Dalriada – modern Argyll and the Inner Hebrides – the Britons of Strathclyde and the Gododdin of the Lothians. The Picts, Britons and the Gododdin are nowadays seen as having been speakers of a P-Celtic tongue, a series of languages or dialects which were related to but distinct from the Q-Celtic Gaelic of the Scots in the west which was close to the similarly Q-Celtic tongues of Ireland and Man. The P-Celtic languages survive in the modern world in Welsh, Breton and the revived Cornish language.

From the various external sources, Roman, Irish, English and Continental we do know of some significant dates concerning the Picts. Although till recently it was thought wise to restrict the use of Picts or Pictish to the period after 297CE [see below p.57] I herein submit that the Picts were effectively the indigenous people(s) of the northern half of Britain. They enter history at the battle of Mons Graupius c.80CE. This battle is reported in a single Roman source but opens a period of Scotland's past where there are limited, but informative, Roman sources delineating their continual and unsuccessful attempts to conquer the northern tribes, and telling us something of the Picts themselves. The Romans left Britain c.409CE and there is no historically accurate information about the Picts for a couple of centuries. By the second half of the seventh century however we enter into a new phase of British history with the expansion of the Northumbrian Angles, and increasingly what little information we can glean about the Picts can be supported from a variety of sources. The great battle between the Northumbrians and the Picts in 685CE, variously known as Nechtansmere or Dunnichen is a key date in that subsequent to this the expansionist policies of Northumbria were doomed to failure. From this time to the eventual creation of the combined Scottish and Pictish Kingdom of Alba in the early 10th century we still lack indigenous source material and there is not a great deal from elsewhere. There is sufficient however to give us a picture of Scotland in the second half of the First Millennium that is open to a variety of interpretations. The vast majority of this material derives from sources created by Christian monks in one way or another and the role of Christianity itself is absolutely central in the societal and political development of the Picts from a tribally structured society to something akin to a nation state, or kingdom. There is enough material, however, to flesh out a clear narrative of who the Picts were and how their society developed, and its fundamental importance in the eventual creation of what we nowadays call Scotland.

At this point I would like to make it clear that I believe, as I have stated elsewhere [McHardy 1997] that our understanding of the past can be greatly enhanced by the critical study of what is generally referred to as folklore. Troy was found because Heinrich Schliemann ignored professional advice from historians and archaeologists and used the 'stories' of Homer to find the location of what was till then considered an imaginary location. Likewise there is much in Scottish tradition that can perhaps be drawn on to help us expand our knowledge of the past. I shall consider particular instances of this variously below, but for those who doubt the practicality of such an approach I recommend consideration of the Diprotodons. The term Diprotodon was coined in the second half of the 20th century to describe prehistoric giant marsupials whose bones and fossils were found in Australia. Ever since the first white man had arrived on the Continent the Dreamtime stories of the aboriginal population concerning these animals had been dismissed as fantasy. The fact is that the indigenous people had carried knowledge of these creatures, through oral transmission, for a period of around 40,000 years [Isaacs 1991]. Story has no brief to tell of precise dates, times and locations but can still tell us much. It can perhaps be used to glean a clearer understanding of our past. If the aboriginal peoples of Australia can hold on to ascertainable facts for 40,000 years it is clearly not beyond possibility that traditions relevant to our understanding of the Picts could have survived in Scotland since the time of the first post-Ice Age settlers.

There is a candidate for just such a tale. It is mentioned by the Christian monk Bede, generally considered the father of English history, who wrote his *History of the English Church and People* in Northumbria in the first quarter of the eighth century. He tells us that

> some Picts, from Scythia, put to sea in a few longships and were driven by the storms around the coasts of Britain, arriving at length on the north coast of Ireland...
>
> [1955, p.38]

This raises an intriguing possibility. Scythia is quite specific and in Bede's time was used to refer to Denmark and southern Scandinavia in general. Can we therefore discern in this tradition the survival of an oral tradition harking back to early settlers who arrived by following the coast of the land that existed in much of what is now the North Sea before 6000BCE? This is well within the bounds of possibility and the Pictish peoples would be truly unique if they possessed no tales of their own origins within their oral traditions.

A further aspect of the value of traditional folklore can be seen in the very name of the Picts, perhaps originally something more like Pecht, which was what they were known as in folklore traditions throughout Scotland well into the 19th century. The term was in use from the

Borders to Shetland and seems to have had the meaning of 'the ancestor peoples'. It was only as universal schooling was established that this term was replaced by Picts, precisely because this, as the term the Romans had used, had become the accepted literary form. As Rivet and Smith suggest in their comments on the term [1979, p.438f], the Romans probably just misheard the real name. The idea that the term Pict is derived from the Roman term *Picti*, supposedly meaning the painted people, does not stand up to scrutiny as Rivet and Smith have shown. The term Pecht, which survived till very late in the oral tradition and in place names, is possibly what they called themselves.

When the Romans arrived in Scotland the population was undoubtedly tribal. It is a telling point that 1,700 years later a considerable part of the country was still essentially the same. The society that existed in the 18th century in much of the Highlands and Islands of Scotland was an anachronism in modern Europe in that the clan system was still, just, a society that was tribal, pastoral, warrior-based and Celtic-speaking, which in itself could be a fair description of the Picts. And I hope I am not alone in hearing an echo of the phrase used by Dio Cassio that these tribes 'were addicted to raiding', in the warnings posted on kirk doors by the British Government in 1746 about the Highland cattle thieves, those members of the Jacobite army of Bonnie Prince Charlie who had refused to surrender and reverted to a combination of traditional cattle-raiding and guerrilla warfare to survive. To this day in many parts of the globe people still live in tribal societies whose daily life is focused round the needs of their cattle, the source of much of their food, the basis of their economy, and certainly throughout Eurasia in prehistoric times the primary focus of inter-tribal raiding. The misreading of Scottish history that has developed has blinded us to the fact that the clans in the Highlands were the descendants of the Picts as well as of the Scots, nor should we forget the role of the Vikings, and as I hope to show, the differentiation of these two groups may well have been little more than the language they spoke. And language is not now, nor has ever been, a badge of ethnicity.

Just because people live in tribes does not mean they are incapable of high levels of organisation. What can be construed as the tyranny of literacy has led us into supposing a level of primitivism always existed amongst pre-literate peoples. The very existence of intricate and sophisticated structures such as Maes Howe, Brodgar, Calanais and the rest from millennia ago shows that the ancestral societies of the tribes of north-west

Europe were not composed of ignorant savages. And of course the Pictish symbols stones are themselves a reminder that the people creating them were great artists. The idea that the 'barbarian' tribes were awaiting the guiding hand of the Roman Empire or the Christian Church to bring them forth from the darkness of ignorance into the light of understanding is an unfortunate interpretation that has underpinned much of our understanding of the past in north-western Europe. Modern western notions of civilization are predicated on urban development and literacy, overlaid with a quasi-religious faith in 'progress', nowadays obsessed with industrialisation and economic development and driven by the profit motive. The state of our planet suggests such faith is misplaced and that there is more to be learned from how our predecessors lived than is generally accepted.

Modern interest in the ancient Pictish peoples of Scotland was both reflected and stimulated by the publication in 1955 of a book called *The Problem of the Picts*. Unfortunately this choice of title has led to a situation where the Picts have continued to be perceived as essentially enigmatic, even unknowable. Hopefully this is no longer the case. Over the past 20 years a series of remarkable about-turns have occurred in our understanding of Scotland's past. That cornerstone of Scottish history, the founding of Dalriada by 'invaders' from Ulster, has been shown by Dr Ewan Campbell [2000] to have no provable foundation at all and the whole concept of the 'Celtic' world has been effectively demolished by Simon James in his *The Atlantic Celts*.

Because of the nature of Scottish historiography to date I believe we are in a position that if we want to create a truly Scottish history of our land we must go back to the basics and 'mak it new'. In this work I am trying to present a cohesive and straightforward narrative of Pictish history. In the course of the book we will consider the Romans, what they had to tell us and how they interrelated with the indigenous tribes; the growth of Northumbria and its effects on the Picts and their neighbours, the Scots and the Britons; their relationships with those neighbours; the arrival and influence of the new Christian religion and how the eventual Pictish state came into existence in relationship to continuing external pressures including the Viking raids from the early ninth century onwards.

Because of this lack of early written indigenous sources, the interpretation of our distant past has always necessitated a considerable deal of speculation. Until we have considerably more archaeological investigation to help us better understand Scotland's past, such speculation must continue and the best I can hope for is that the reader considers my suggestions and interpretations as being at least informed speculation. There is an old cliché about the past being another country – when that country is described according to the history of another society it can hardly hope to fit. The ideas presented herein are mine and if they are felt to be wrong-headed, or even offensive, the blame too is mine, and mine alone.

Note on Spelling and References

In recent times it has become academic practice to use spellings for the names of people and places in First Millennium Scotland in forms close to those in the oldest surviving documents. For the sake of clarity, while I have left such spelling in quoted works, the general approach in the text is to follow the earlier simplified spelling as used in Anderson's *Early Sources of Scottish History*. The use of Celtic in this work will be restricted to discussion of language, always bearing in mind that even that designation is no older than the 18th century. Quotations use the Harvard system where the book referred to is given by author and publication date as given in the Bibliography, followed by page reference. There are also quotes from Web sources for which the URL site description is given in the Bibliography.

CHAPTER ONE

Tribal Scotland

THE ROMANS ARRIVED IN Scotland *c.*80CE having conquered much of Europe and subdued the peoples of England. Over the next four centuries as the *Pax Romana* held sway in those areas, the Roman Empire was obliged to maintain a defensive wall to keep out the peoples to the north. Who were these people and why did they continue to be a threat to the mighty Roman Empire? In order to answer these questions we have to rely on a combination of various types of source material. The only surviving written material from the period comes from Roman sources but we also have the archaeological record and as I hope I have shown [McHardy 1997] we can also call on some of the traditional stories pertaining to these early peoples to try and gain a greater understanding of who they were and how they lived. Before concerning ourselves with the variety of peoples then living in Scotland, we should consider some other matters. What type of society was in existence? Was it essentially indigenous or was it a development based on relatively recent immigration?

What seems abundantly clear from a variety of Roman sources is that the peoples in Scotland were, like the whole of Britain 130 years earlier, essentially tribal. Caesar had said

> The interior of Britain is inhabited by tribes who claim, on the strength of an oral tradition, to be aboriginal...
>
> [Caesar V, 12 URL]

This may be compared with what Bede had to say about the origins of the Picts some eight centuries later regarding their arrival from Scythia [above p.17]. As we shall see below the importance of Ireland in Scottish history has been overstated, but the key point here is that Bede says that this was 'according to tradition'. We know that in his time Scythia was not used to refer to the area that the Greeks and Romans meant, which was north of the Black Sea, but to the area of Europe that we nowadays think of as Scandinavia.

Elsewhere Bede tells us that the first people in Britain had come in from the south but here we perhaps have a reference to an arrival from the east. We should consider whether this might in fact be a tradition, or folk-tale, that had survived from a time when the North Sea had not yet formed and thus might refer to arrivals along the coast of the land bridge that existed where the North Sea now is. This land bridge did not disappear till c.6000BCE and the survival of accurate reporting through storytelling for 40,000 years in Australia already referred to [Isaacs 1991], would support the possibility that this could be a tale from that period. In the far distant past even though people seem to have been able to travel considerable distances over the open sea in skin boats, the preferred method of such travel would probably have been along coastal routes. Bede's reference to longships is anachronistic but travelling along coastal routes in skin boats even as early as the seventh millennium BCE is not beyond possibility. As Cunliffe has shown [2001 *passim*] the old concept of the sea being a barrier to prehistoric peoples is contradicted absolutely by the archaeological record. In fact travel by sea was until relatively recently in human history a much easier form of transport than travelling overland. This continued to be true in most of Scotland which never had an extensive network of metalled roads till very late. The efficiency of sea travel and consequent easy communication is something which itself suggests a specific political interpretation of the development of Scotland as a nation, as we shall see later. Bede also tells us that the Picts first went to Ireland and asked permission to settle, a request which was refused, and it was recommended they move to Scotland. He goes on to tell us that the Picts had no women of their own and that they asked the Scots there for wives, before crossing to Scotland. This makes little sense as Scotland was inhabited at least as early as Ireland was, and the reference to wives has been interpreted as some kind of reference to the much discussed Pictish system of matrilineal succession. In matrilineal systems, rights, power and status pass down through the female line from mother to daughter. Patrilineal systems, which have been dominant in many parts of the world for a considerable time, see such inheritance as passing from father to son. Western scholarship has long assumed that primogeniture, the passing of rights and possessions from father to son is the 'natural' form of human society. In fact both systems are known throughout history, but Campbell notes that Bede in telling us of the origin of the Scots follows the well-worn path of

... origin legends of a type common to most peoples of the period, constructed to show the descent of a ruling dynasty from a powerful, mythical or religious figure. Such genealogies could be, and often were, manipulated to suit the political climate of the time...

[Campbell 2000, p.288]

As we shall see Bede's further statement that the Scots emigrated into Argyll from Ireland has no contemporary evidence to sustain it and we must be careful not to depend too much on any source that has little or no contemporary support. The idea that any tribal people migrated without their womenfolk makes no sense at all. This may have made sense on raiding expeditions but not where settlement was the aim. When it comes to his own times however, as we shall see, Bede does tell us much of significance.

Strabo, Tacitus and others all refer to the indigenous peoples as living in tribes while Dio Cassio refers to two main tribes, and Ptolemy, the second century Roman geographer, famously refers to a total of 18 different tribes on his map of North Britain.

The definition of a tribe according to the Compact Oxford English Dictionary (1979) is:

a   A group of persons forming a community and claiming descent from a common ancestor
b   A particular race of recognised ancestry; a family.

This I suggest is the key to understanding First Millennium Scotland. Tribes function in specific ways and in Scotland we had a tribal society that survived into the 18th century, which, being descended directly from the tribal peoples of the First Millennium, can provide us with a possible model for understanding earlier society. The description of the Highland clans as Celtic-speaking, economically self-sufficient, mainly pastoral, warrior societies gives us a clear picture of the society surviving into the 18th century. However such a description would also appear to be a good fit for the society that the Romans encountered when they came north. Tribal societies are built round the kin-group. Everyone knows exactly how they are related to everyone else and the fact that they are descended from a common ancestor – or even that they claim to be – means that any hierarchy within such societies is the very antithesis of society formed round the differentiation between aristocratic élites and the rest of society. There is a level of egalitarianism in such societies that is based directly on the blood link between their members. Dio Cassio referred to them thus:

> Their form of rule is democratic for the most part, and they are fond of plundering; consequently they choose their boldest men as rulers.
>
> [1927, p.264]

I would suggest that by stating them to be democratic he misunderstands the egalitarianism of such tribes. The chiefs of the later Highland clans had no feudal right of primogeniture and there was always at least the possibility of a level of elective process in their selection. Chiefs could even be deposed if they were not thought to be up to the job. [Scott 1893, p.47] This makes sense in a society formed around blood-relationships. Given the structure of late Highland society: warrior tribes claiming descent from a single eponymous ancestor, living in a mainly pastoral economy and like their ancestors 'addicted to raiding', I believe we can gain some insight as to how society functioned when the Romans arrived by looking at the clan system, which appears to have been, in broad outline, little different from the Iron Age society from which it had originally developed. The centrality of the warrior tradition and the practice of cattle raiding are in themselves clear markers of this as I have noted elsewhere [McHardy 2004]. While there is no doubt that there were tyrants amongst clan chiefs at different times, the very fact that each individual is conceived as being a relation of the chief means that the chief has a complex web of responsibilities and duties towards his own kin as well as a range of specific rights and privileges. To illustrate this one need only consider the Highland clan chiefs custom of 'ostentation'. The chiefs were always resplendent when seen outside their own territory or when receiving visitors. They would be clad in lace and silk and their weapons and accoutrements would have trimmings of silver and gold while their clansmen were uniformly dressed in simple tartan cloth. This clearly differentiated the chief from his kin, but not as an aristocrat was separated from the peasantry. It was a matter of honour for all members of a particular clan that their chief was at least as richly dressed, if not more so, than the chief of any other clan. The chief's central role in a society which was in its essentials based on self-sufficiency reflected back on the whole of his kin, i.e. the entire clan. Burt commented on clan society in the 1730s thus:

Their submission to their chiefs has been called slavish; and too many of the chiefs of the present day are willing enough to have this believed, because they wish to impute their own want of influence to any cause rather than the true one; but the lowest clansman felt his own individual importance as much as his chief, whom he considered as such only *ad vitam aut ad culpam* [so long as good behaviour lasts] and although there was certainly a strong feeling in favour of the lineal descendant of the steam-father of their race, which prevented them from being rash, harsh, or unjust to him, there was also a strong feeling of honour and independence, which prevented them from being unjust to themselves. When a chief proved unworthy of his rank, he was degraded from it, and (to avoid jealousy and strife) the next in order was constituted in his room – but never a low-born man or a stranger; as it was a salutary rule among them, as in other military establishments, not to put one officer over the head of another. But it was not with a Highland chief as with other rulers; 'When *he* fell, he fell like Lucifer, never to rise again'; his degradation was complete, because he owed it to a common feeling of reprobation, not to the caprice, malice, or ambition of a faction; for every one was thoroughly acquainted with the merits of the cause, and while there was any thing to be said in his favour, his people had too much respect for themselves to show public disrespect to him. The same dignified feeling prevented their resentment from being bloody; he was still their kinsman, however unworthy; and having none among them to take his part, was no longer dangerous.

[Burt 1981, xl–xli]

While this comparison may at first seem of little relevance to the First Millennium, consider the following. When Tacitus describes the battle of Mons Graupius he says:

... one of the many leaders, named Calgacus, a man of outstanding valour and nobility, summoned the masses who were already
thirsting for battle and addressed them...

[30, p.79]

He does not call him a king, a count or an emperor, simply one of many
leaders and a man of outstanding valour and nobility, but without call-
ing him a noble. He appears to have held his role an account of his skill
rather than any supposed particular birthright or aristocratic position.
This again is echoed in later clan society where each clan had its own
captain who led them into battle. It would be a strange family indeed
that would put its own lives at risk by having anyone other than the
most martially talented man to lead them into battle. However the chief,
or the possible candidates for chieftainship, would certainly have to
prove themselves as warriors, a process that has long antecedents. Thus,
from Ginzburg's *Ecstasies,*

In the legendary biography of the young hero, the theft of live-
stock carried out in league with their contemporaries was an
obligatory stage, virtually an initiation ritual. It respected a very
ancient mythical model, amply documented in the Indo-European
cultural milieu...

[1990, p.236]

Cattle raiding was a central part of ancient tribal activity throughout
Eurasia, and it maintained this centrality in Scotland into the 18th century
[McHardy 2004 *passim*]. Calgacus' name has been suggested as meaning
'the swordsman', which is a good name for a warrior but not necessarily
for what we nowadays think of as a king, particularly in a society where
it appears that all men were warriors. Further to this, the oldest surviving
poem in Welsh, *The Gododdin*, which was written at the dawn of the
seventh century in the Lothians, can perhaps help our understanding. It
has generally been interpreted as referring to 'an aristocratic warrior
society' but this is not really supported by the text itself. Each of the 60
verses follows the same pattern and describes the valour of the warrior
concerned. There are few references to rank and as John T Koch points
out the existence of a 'king' directing the proceedings is based on a misreading of the text. The two words *mynydowc mwynvawr* have in the

past been interpreted as referring to a king, in Dun Eidyn or Edinburgh, but this is not supported in the text. Koch points out there are no references to the presence of such a person in the battle at Catraeth which is the subject of the poem, and no reference either to his parentage or his death. He goes on,

> At first view *mynydowc mwynvawr* are a pair of transparently intelligible adjectives... meaning respectively 'mountainous' or 'of the mountains' and 'having great wealth'. Throughout the elegies these glosses yield adequate sense without being invested with personhood; thus referring suitably, say, to the combined aristocratic forces of the northern highland zone, the mountain feast, perhaps sometimes to the luxurious mountain chief, the luxurious mountain country, the luxurious mountain court or hall.'
>
> (Koch 1997, xlvi)

I would contend that there is no good reason to assume that these warriors are in any way aristocratic and that it is anachronistic to think of them as such within tribal society. The idea of the luxurious mountain court or hall is one which I suggest would be a good fit. All tribal societies at all times have had councils of one sort or another and it would be of particular importance to hold one before going into battle or going off on a raid. The whole tenor of the Gododdin suggests that the warriors are an élite gathering, but this I propose would be more likely to have been because of their battle skills rather than anything to do with any accidental status of their birth.

Another pointer to the nature of contemporary society in First Millennium Scotland comes from Dalriada, which appears to have been a Q-Celtic speaking society parallel to the P-Celtic speaking societies of Strathclyde, Lothian and further north, and not an incoming colony from Ulster. There are repeated references in early sources to the Cenel Gabhran, Cenel Loarn and Cenel Angus. These are clearly specific examples of the normal tribal practice of claiming common descent from a single ancestor, Cenel appearing to mean roughly the same as the later term clan. These tribes seem to have been just as indigenous as those mentioned by Ptolemy. Campbell tell us that

... if there was a mass migration from Ireland to Scotland, there should be some sign of this in the archaeological record, but there is none. If there was only an élite takeover by a war band, who must have adopted local material culture and settlement forms, there should be signs of the language of the native majority in the place names, but again there is none.

[2001, p.290]

Later clan chiefs had to be of the direct line of descent from the claimed ancestor and the model of kin-based warrior society is clear here. In this respect we should also perhaps consider the terminology used to describe the leaders of such societies. The word *righ* in Gaelic is generally translated as a king or governor [MacLennan 1925, p.269] while in Welsh *rhi* is translated as king, lord. Given the influence of the Bible and Classical studies on all early extant written materials from the British Isles, it is hardly surprising that such materials refer to societal leaders as kings but I suggest we would be better thinking of these early tribal leaders as chiefs, even high-chiefs rather than kings or high kings. The term king has strong connotations of feudalism and the tribal form of society has little in common with feudalism other than a shared basic military structure. In clan society each able-bodied man was a warrior and obliged to come to the defence of the clan when summoned [Scott, Logan]. He was not in thrall to someone higher up the social scale, though he would follow his clan chief or captain to the death. Each individual warrior was responsible to himself and to the clan under the leadership of the chief and whoever was leading them into battle, or more often on raids. As already noted, I have written elsewhere of the centrality of the raiding tradition in Highland society [McHardy 2003], and I suggest that we have a specific Pictish reference to this practice. This is the Dull stone which shows warriors both on foot and on horseback accompanied by dogs. The presence of dogs strongly suggests that what we have here is a raid setting out to 'lift' cattle from another tribe or clan. That some warriors are mounted and some on foot might reflect either different levels of wealth – not uncommon even in families – or possibly that there were different roles to be played in the course of the raid by the mounted warriors and those on foot; after all the combination of cavalry and infantry is an ancient and universal feature of military activity.

Ptolemy's map of Britain compiled in the second century CE lists tribes from various parts of Scotland. These were given by Watson [1993, p.15] as Caerini, Cornavii, Lugi, Smertae, Decantae, Carnonacae, Caledonii, Vacomagi, Taexali, Venicones, Creones, Epidii, Damnonii, Novantae, Selgovae and Votadini, several of which tribal names find echo in later times. The Votadini of Ptolemy have been recognised as the predecessors of the Gododdin of south-east Scotland and there have been suggestions that the Selgovae are remembered in the place name Selkirk. Different Roman sources give variations of some of these names; Ammianus Marcelinus refers to Dicalydones and Verturiones, and the former term contains the term Caledonian which appears to have been used as both a generic term for all of the tribal peoples of Scotland by several writers and as a specific group in Glen Albyn by Ptolemy. Both the forms Damnonii and Cornavii are close to tribal names that were used in the south of Britain, something which may well have also been true of the Decantae. However, one of the other names provides yet another possible example of continuity. This is the Epidii, a name stated by WJ Watson to be derived from *epos* [1993, p.23] meaning horse and perhaps linked to Epona, a horse goddess among the Gauls. They are specifically located in Kintyre where later the MacEacherns, or sons of the horsemen, were later to be found. That this might be more than just the handing down of a name is suggested by a singular event in the Jacobite rebellion of 1715. The brother of the Duke of Argyll had assembled a force of troops at Inverary to counteract the growing Jacobite army at Perth. A party of MacEacherns came to join him bringing with them a considerable number of horses, as back-up for the cavalry who were part of the army. Here again we see a link between 18th century Scotland and the First Millennium, underlining precisely the fact that much of Scottish society was rooted in practices inherited from as far back as the Iron Age.

Societies whose main form of moveable wealth is cattle tend to be societies where inter-tribal raiding is endemic. Dio Cassio's 'fond of plundering' finds a strange echo in 18th century Scotland where the Jacobites who stayed out after Culloden were described in Government documents as 'thieves'. [Simpson 1926, p.73] The reason cattle were traditionally plundered was precisely because they were the accepted expression of moveable wealth and their central importance to pastoral societies, such as the Romans encountered when they arrived in Scotland, is clear.

As Ginzburg noted (*supra*) this type of activity was, or had been, common throughout Eurasia in pre-urban societies and this raises the point that while much of Europe had been forcibly changed under the influence of the Roman Empire over the two centuries previous to Agricola's arrival, in Scotland things were probably much as they had been elsewhere in earlier times. The society the Romans encountered at the end of the first century CE was a direct development of earlier indigenous society. Thankfully nowadays we are no longer in thrall to the concept of societal change always occurring as a result of military invasion. Historical categorisation of prehistoric times is not always an aid to understanding. As Armit and Ralston put it,

> The Iron Age is increasingly seen as one chronological slice within a longer period stretching from the Later Bronze Age to the emergence of the Pictish and Scottish states, and the Viking incursions of around 800. Already apparent in studies undertaken in the 1970s (e.g. Thoms 1980), this perspective has been reinforced by the recent concentration of research on Atlantic Scotland: the absence of a significant Roman interlude in the North and West has buttressed the adoption of this wider time-frame. Although terminology to replace the classic chronological sequence (Iron Age – Roman – early Historic) has yet to be developed for other parts of Scotland, there is little dissent among present students of Iron Age Scotland that the Roman incursions may have been less disruptive to the development of native societies than was once proposed...
>
> [2003, p.174]

As yet we have no archaeological evidence for any large scale invasion of the northern parts of Britain before the Romans and, short of finding any, it seems that we are entitled to presume that the peoples the Romans called Picts were in fact the indigenous population of this part of the world within that wider time-frame. While it would be simplistic to suggest that this was the case in every specific locale, in general terms we are justified in perceiving the Picts as being the contemporary representatives of that indigenous population on the arrival of the Romans. The reference to a Scythian origin (supra), meaning Scandinavia, would fit in with the idea of at least some of the original, hunter-gatherer population of the northern half of the British Isles as having come in over the land bridge as the land gradually became capable of sustaining human communities in the post-Ice Age period. This would thus suggest that the Picts were at least partially descended from those people and their descendants who later built the megalithic structures, which themselves are a clear example of the reality that people in this part of the British Isles were never isolated from what was going on in the rest of the world. The spread of megalithic culture in fact might as well be posited as having originated in perhaps Orkney and spreading south, as having originated elsewhere and come north. The invasion theory should perhaps be joined in the dustbin of past-their-sell-by-date historical theories by the Mediterranean-centred interpretations of our past, that are a result of the effects of literacy having developed there earlier than here, and thus giving rise to an unfortunate, if to some extent understandable, respect for what is still thought of as Classical culture, i.e. the products of Greco–Romano civilisation. The idea that non-urban, pre-literate society is inferior to urban literate societies is at its root every bit as offensive as blatant racism. Its assumptions also lead to a kind of cultural blindness which I suggest is linked to the idea that history must be defined by written sources alone. The well-known instance of the German industrialist Schliemann finding Troy, in the face of derision from archaeologists and historians, by following the 'stories' told in Homer's *Iliad* illustrates there are other ways of interpreting the past than reliance on the written word alone. Pre-literate peoples are neither necessarily primitive nor crude. This is perhaps why we have had so much paper and ink used up in trying to decide from whom the Picts learned how to carve stone. If they were the direct descendants of the people who raised the megaliths, they were heir to millennia of stone working. And we should also remember the great number of cup and ring sites around Scotland, dating from as early as the Fourth Millennium BCE, which suggest some sort of ritual behaviour. There are also at least a couple of possible examples of early animal representations. These are of deer at Ballochmyle and Glen Domhain. The Picts too sculpted deer and we must consider the possibility of a continuum of symbolic usage of such images.

Although few Pictish symbols are found on Stone or Bronze Age sites there are a couple of notable exceptions. Douglas C Scott has pointed out that the three Aberlemno roadside stones form a clear solar alignment which he has dated to at least as early as the Bronze Age [Scott 2003].

There is also a Pictish symbol on the Edderton stone in Easter Ross [*Ibid*] which is likewise part of an alignment. The continuance of usage of earlier sacred sites is well attested. It was deliberate Christian policy to take over the pagan precincts as Bede attests. In a letter from Pope Gregory to Bishop Mellitus in 601CE we find the following,

> ... destroy the idols, but the temples themselves are to be aspersed with holy water, altars set up, and relics enclosed within them. For if these temples are well built, they are to be purified from devil-worship, and dedicated to the service of the true God.
>
> [1955, p.86]

This is explicit and we should not be surprised at Bede's inability to see the irony in re-using such sites, making them acceptable by replacing the idols with relics. Is it this deliberate Christian policy that gave rise to the widespread location of early churches in Scotland being erected on mounds? Later we shall consider the possibility that such mounds are likely to have been the foci of a wide range of communal behaviour in the years before the arrival of Christianity and were therefore sacred sites themselves. This might also be a contributory factor to the widespread location of Pictish symbol stones at Christian churches. Just as story can survive language change so it seems that ritual sites can survive major shifts in social behaviour resulting from new practices in ritual and belief. The above quote from Armit and Ralston in its reference to the wider time-frame can be seen as incorporating the possibility of just such a continuity of usage of these types of sites, particularly if there are grounds for seeing possible parallel continuities in belief systems – a point to which we will return.

In pre-literate societies throughout the world one of the recurring aspects of sacral behaviour is a reverence towards the ancestors and therefore a consequent respect for locations associated with them, such as earlier sacred sites, tombs, barrows, etc. The re-usage of hilltop sites, no longer being exclusively interpreted as of military importance, may well be another instance of the same sort of process. Elsewhere I have considered the putative location of priestess groups on specific notable hilltop sites as representing a long term continuity in belief [McHardy 2003, 2006]. It would therefore appear worthwhile to consider whether the occurrence of Pictish Symbols at sites dated much earlier than the First Millennium CE can be interpreted as a sign of just such a continuity.

By this interpretation then, the Picts can be seen not just as the contemporaries of the Romans, but effectively as the indigenous population of Scotland since prehistoric times. Smyth suggested [1984, p.44] that we should see the Pictish period as opening with the battle of Mons Graupius. I contend we should rather see the Picts themselves as being the indigenous population and should therefore not qualify their temporal relevance by reference to external history.

It is also important to realise that the Picts were not isolated from contemporary European society. Cultural relationships with mainland Europe existed from an early period. In describing the timber-built hall at Balbridie dated to c.3,500BCE Oram tells us that it

... appears to be related to house forms found on early Neolithic sites in Holland and Germany

[1997, p.24]

and later in the same work refers to 'sunflower' pins that are closely related to similar ones from northern Germany, telling us that:

Similar links between northern Germany and the north-east of Scotland are suggested by a localised group of later 8th century to 7th century BCE items named for the site of Covesea, or in hoards from Braes of Gight and Glentanar in Aberdeenshire and Balmashanner at Forfar in Angus, have been used as arguments in favour of at least close trading links with the north German plain and southern Scandinavia if not a localised movement of colonists.

[Ibid, p.67]

Such a putative movement of colonists would of course have been just as likely in the other direction. Given Bede's reference to incomers from Scythia and the fact that regular contacts between Scotland and these areas have continued through historical and into modern times we can at the least postulate that Picts were, like their ancestors and their descendants, in ongoing, if perhaps sporadic, contact with tribal peoples in northern Europe. Such contacts are not just of cultural significance but have a political aspect that may well have been of some influence during the latter years of Roman occupation of southern Britain.

The name of the Picts

An ongoing topic of study and discussion in dealing with the Picts has been not just what period of our history within which can we reliably use the name, but what the name itself represents. Having already made the case that material from the oral tradition can be of assistance in helping us to understand our past [McHardy 1997] I would like to consider the term for the Picts that survives in such tradition. The term in general use from the Borders to Shetland was Pecht or Pegh. It is clear from the allocation of the name to a diverse and temporally broad spectrum of sites including prehistoric tumuli to medieval deer-dykes [McHardy 1992] that the term Pecht was used as general catch-all term for 'the ancestors' within Scotland. Both the name itself and its geographical spread are of significance. Rivet and Smith [1979, p.438] pointed out that they considered the name that occurs in the seventh century Ravenna Cosmography – derived from a list of Antonine Forts that originated in the second century – was a version of a tribal name akin to Pecht. They further note that the neighbouring peoples of the Picts, whether Celtic or Germanic speaking, all used forms that were Pe- rather than Pi-. Nicolaisen makes the following point:

> The Roman Picts corresponds closely to the Old Norse Péttir... and to the Old English Pehtas, Pihtas, Pyhtas, Peohtas, and Piohtas of the Anglo-Saxon Chronicle (as well as the first elements of the personal names Peohthelm, Peohtred, Peohtweald, Peohtwine, Peohtwulf, etc.) and there is little doubt that these linguistic variants do not derive from each other but from a common source – probably a native name...
>
> [1976, p.151]

It is also important to note that the first dated reference to the Picts in 297CE is a retrospective one, referring to them as having been among the tribal peoples with whom Julius Caesar battled c.55BCE. It seems clear that the people we nowadays refer to as Picts had a name similar to this and that they were the indigenous people of Scotland. This clearly shows that it is highly unlikely that they were given their name by the Romans, and therefore the idea of the term meaning 'the painted ones' has no basis in fact. We should now consider just who the Romans were referring to as *Picti*.

The first recorded mention of indigenous tribes refer to them as Caledonians, a term that has been generally accepted as having the meaning of the 'people of the woods'. The term is used by Strabo, Pliny the Elder, Tacitus and Martial in the first century CE and subsequently by Dio Cassius and Solinus before the first surviving use of the term Pict. However in the ensuing centuries it is clear that the terms Caledonian and Pict are effectively interchangeable as general descriptions of the tribal peoples of North Britain, even though Ptolemy specifically locates the Caledones in the area of the Great Glen. For the past century and more both the Picts and the Caledonians have been accepted as living north of the Forth–Clyde line, despite widespread acceptance that the Caledonian Forest itself stretched to the Borders. The putative division of the Picts into northern and southern divisions or kingdoms has likewise been generally accepted, with the Caledonians being considered as inhabiting the lands north of the Tay and the Maetae, mentioned as early as the second century living between there and the Forth–Clyde line. This is a misreading of the original source. Dio Cassius says explicitly

> There are two principal tribes of the Britons, the Caledonii and the Maeatae, and the names of the others have been merged in these two. The Maeatae live next to the cross-wall which cuts the island in half, and the Caledonians are beyond them...
>
> [1927, p.263]

He is writing about the Severan campaign of the early years of the second century and most commentators have assumed that he is referring to the northern Antonine Wall. The Severan campaigns did not conclude till around 211 and Dio Cassius did not write this section of his history till 217 at the earliest [Millar 1964, p.194]. Recent excavations of the Antonine Wall have made a significant point regarding dating:

> The latest coin from an excavation on an Antonine Wall fort, a denarus of Luculla dating from 164+, found in a granary of the supply-base of Old Kilpatrick, the westernmost fort on the wall

could well date (or provide a *terminus post quem* for) the activities of the final demolition parties on that frontier.

[Swan 1999, p.448]

This is 50 years before Dio Cassius is writing his history and given his access to contemporary sources and to people who had been on the northern frontier with Severus, it seems highly unlikely he was referring to the Antonine Wall. While the fact that Severus re-built some of the forts along the line of the old Antonine Wall is undeniable, the reference is specifically to 'the Wall that divides the island in half'. Given the period when he was writing, I contend that Dio Cassius was referring to Hadrian's Wall and that the tribes merged into the Maetae were in fact the Votadini, Selgovae and Damnonii of Ptolemy, and possibly also the Novantae in the south-west. Whether the Venicones of Fife were part of the Caledonian or the Maetae confederations in this reading is moot. Scholars have too often allowed the modern, rigidly defined borders of the nation state to influence how they see the past. We are dealing with tribal peoples, who although fiercely defensive of what they considered their own territory were not members of such a nation state.

Much has been made of the place name Dumyat in the eastern Ochils, as meaning the fort of the Maetae. Wainwright tells us

In point of fact there is good reason to believe that Dumyat and Myot Hill stood within a few miles of the southern boundary of the Maetae.

[1955, p.24]

This hilltop site overlooks the northern bank of the Forth which is a notable geographical boundary and may well have marked the *northern* limits of Maetae territory on my reading. There is also an alternative explanation to these place names being within the homeland of the Maetae, or Miathi as they are later called by Adomnan. Eastern Scotland is full of instances of the place names Inglistoun and Scotstoun, both of which refer to settlements, of whatever temporal extent, of people not considered indigenous to the area. This is particularly notable in the Scotstoun forms, the existence of which suggests they might well pre-cede the coalition of the Picts and the Scots in the later ninth century. A further example suggests that such settlements, perhaps of groups of warriors from other tribes, were possible. This is Rathillet in Fife, which is accepted as meaning the Fort of the Ulstermen, the use of the Irish term *rath* underlining this [Watson 1993, p.239]. Given that in early First Millennium Scotland we are dealing with societies which were much less rigidly structured than nation states, it is possible that such settlements were a normal part of such society. The extent of the Inglistoun and Scotstoun names would suggest it. Fordun in the *Scotichronicon* writes of a group of young Pictish warriors in residence at the Scottish capital in Dalriada [Watt 1993, Vol 1 p.265]. Given the fluidity of tribal relationships and our lack of precise understanding of contemporary society, it may be that what we perceive of as natural borders were not that rigid, or even that some of the tribes that Dio Cassius perceived as belonging to the federation of the Maetae, did inhabit lands north of the Forth. The substantive point however is that he is referring to southern Scotland as their locale.

In order to better understand what the situation amongst these tribal peoples was, it is perhaps worth remembering that the amalgamation of the tribes against the invading Romans in 80AD at Mons Graupius suggests a society which, although accustomed to intra-tribal raiding, was capable of putting aside day-to-day differences in the face of a common enemy. Such a flexibility finds an echo in the later clan times when such confederations as Siol Alpin and Clan Chattan incorporated a diverse range of kin groups. We also have the situation in the mid-18th century where clans who regularly raided each other united within the Jacobite army of Prince Charles Edward Stewart.

Although we have no dated Roman usage of the word Pict before 297 that has survived, to whom did they think they were referring? It appears possible then, if not probable, that the terms Caledonians and Picts were used to describe all of the peoples living in what we now call Scotland. As already noted this would include the Scots, whose supposed arrival in Argyll *c.*500 has been shown to have no contemporary support, historical, linguistic or archaeological. In fact Campbell goes so far as to say

My reading of the archaeological, historical and linguistic evidence is radically different from the traditional account, but much simpler.
I suggest that the people inhabiting Argyll maintained a regional identity from at least the Iron Age through to the

medieval period and that throughout this period they were Gaelic speakers. In this maritime province, sea communications dominated, and allowed a shared archaic language to be maintained, isolated from linguistic developments which were taking place in the areas of Britain to the east of the Highland massif in the Late Roman period.

[2000, p.291]

We should also consider the following. Dalriada, with its capital Dunadd, is in the middle of what is now known as Kilmartin Glen. This is one of the richest archaeological areas in Europe, its standing stones, alignments, cairns, chambered cairns and extensive rock art clearly pointing to the fact that Kilmartin had been the focus of significant sacred activity for thousands of years. If we accept Campbell's thesis that the Scots did not originate in Ulster then they would have to be indigenous. If they were, then they were the custodians of a remarkable sacred tradition already thousands of years old before the Romans came to our island. This ancient sacred centre would have presented problems for the incoming Christian missionaries. It is surely no coincidence that Columba became so involved with Dalriada. Even if the specific activities associated with the oldest of the Kilmartin sites, dating from at least as far back as the Fourth Millennium BCE, had changed or even died out, the sheer extent of the sites in Kilmartin Glen suggests they must have had some role within the culture of the Scots, and conceivably within the wider tribal society of Scotland and of at least the northern area of Ireland. For the new religion to triumph the old one had to be suppressed and what better way to do it than suggest that the Scots, who appear likely to have been the preservers of a remarkable continuity of sacred activities centred round the plethora of sites in Kilmartin Glen, were recent incomers, thus rupturing that continuity and deflecting interest away from the old ways. With the introduction of literacy this interpretation may well have wiped out anything that existed within the oral culture of the indigenous people referring to such beliefs.

In the forthcoming book on the early symbols of the Picts I will look further into the possibilities of the make-up of the pre-Christian religion in Scotland but as far as Kilmartin Glen is concerned it seems fair to suggest that, given the extent and antiquity of the sacred landscape here, that it would have been known on much more than a local scale. The point made previously that Picts was a term used by the Romans to designate all the tribal peoples of Scotland reinforces the necessity of looking at this period of Scottish history not in terms of the later political developments that led to the different polities of Dalriada, Pictland and Strathclyde, but in terms of a society in which kin-groups were dominant.

The first mention of the Scots in history is of course as allies of the Picts fighting against the Romans in the late fourth century. From what the various Roman sources tell us of Scotland at this time it is clear that there were no towns or cities of any note. However it is notable that a number of prominent hills, which would appear to have been the focus of communal sacral activities such as the fire-festivals of Beltain and Samhain [McNeill 1959, Chap viii; 1961, Chap i] seem to have been the focus of Roman activity in that they have Roman camps close to them [McHardy 2001, p.149]. This can be explained by the Romans being aware that such sites were of central importance for the local tribe or tribes, in that they were used regularly for such communal activities as religious rites, important social activities, the dispensation of law and perhaps even annual allocation of lands amongst the community. In the absence of cities or towns such sites would provide focal points that the Romans could comprehend as being of considerable significance. By the time the Romans arrived in the northern half of the British Isles they had already overrun most of Europe and had developed a methodology of conquest and control. The lack of clearly defined central locales as seats of political power was perhaps part of the ongoing problem they had in trying to subdue this part of the world. Again a comparison can be made with late Highland society where towns were virtually unknown in the Highlands outside of Inverness, Inverary, Dingwall and a handful of others, precisely because the clan folk lived in small clachans, collections of houses each occupied by a handful of families, scattered throughout the straths and glens 'without walls or cities' as Dio Cassius had said of their ancestors. It is a standard part of military occupation to take over important political and/or military centres but given the scattered nature of indigenous society and that the entire male population were warriors, this would not have been of much use to the Roman attempts to command and control Scotland.

Since the 17th century a great deal of effort has gone into the study of the Celtic languages. It is generally accepted that the Picts, the Gododdin of Lothian and the Britons of Strathclyde spoke a P-Celtic form, while the Scots in Argyll spoke a Q-Celtic language. Linguists suggest they were originally dialects of the same tongue, splitting eventually into P-Celtic which survives in modern Welsh and Breton, and Q-Celtic, which developed into modern Scots Gaelic and Irish. However this fascination with language has, I suggest, led to a misreading of the period. The nature of tribal society is that one is bound by rights and duties to one's immediate kin and beyond them to the tribe. Notions of linguistic or national identity would be totally anachronistic in such societies. The idea of some concept of pan-Celticism amongst tribal peoples speaking languages that were not defined as being 'Celtic' till modern times has been shown to be anachronistic by Professor James [1999]. The modern usage of the term Celtic which mistakenly applies it to people speaking Celtic languages as if it had some ethnic meaning is no older than the 18th century, and would have meant absolutely nothing to the inhabitants of Britain in the First Millennium. People understood their place in the world as part of an established kin-group living in a specific territory. Their world view was bounded by their duties, obligations, and rights within the immediate family and the wider kin-group. And as we have seen there are no good reasons for seeing the various tribes or groups of tribes as being other than the direct descendants of earlier peoples and perhaps even of the first post-Ice Age peoples, intermingled with a variety of incoming settlers at different times [Sykes 2006 *passim*].

On the principle that the simplest idea is usually the best I therefore suggest that when the Romans came here they saw in the Caledonians or Picts a variety of different tribes, living in small kin-groups with a subsistence economy, who were much like other societies they had met during their conquest of Europe and elsewhere. Many of the Roman troops, particularly among the auxiliaries, would have been brought up in similar societies and they would have not expected anything other than victory over them. Scotland however was to Rome over the succeeding centuries as Afghanistan was to the British Empire, and continues to be to the aspiring New World Order of American neo-cons and their subservient British supporters. It was an area whose peoples resisted all efforts to command and control them. And to the Romans the peoples north of Hadrian's Wall were of a piece, whether called Caledonian or Pict. And the tribes to the north looking south saw a society that had changed utterly in a couple of centuries, had raised a great stone wall against them and had sent repeated invasions north to try and conquer them. No matter what relationship there had been between the tribes of the north and their cousins to the south, once the latter were under Roman rule they were the enemy. In fact the Roman incursions into Scotland set a pattern that continued until modern times and was only ended by the somewhat controversial political union of 1707.

CHAPTER TWO

The Romans march north

THE FIRST DATEABLE REFERENCE to the indigenous people of northern Britain that we have is from Tacitus in *The Agricola*. Tacitus was a Roman writer who was the son-in-law of Agricola, governor of Britain in the second half of the first century CE. The work was written to celebrate the life of his father-in-law and as the first written evidence of life in Scotland it is of great importance. However we should remember that in Tacitus we have a Roman who never, as far as it is known, visited Scotland, and was thus reporting second hand. Additionally we have to remember that the modern idea of history – where it is supposed to aspire to some form of objectivity – would have meant little to Tacitus and what we nowadays class as propaganda was perfectly acceptable to contemporary Roman society. As there are no other known references to the battle of Mons Graupius which takes up a large part of the work, we cannot even be absolutely sure that it took place as described, or even at all. After all what better for a heroic Roman like Agricola than to be portrayed as having scored a remarkable victory against the barbarian hordes? To this day the location of this putative battle continues to exert a strange fascination for amateur and professional historians in Scotland. Though the Romans never did conquer Scotland, their ongoing struggles with the indigenous peoples are clearly of the utmost importance.

Tacitus tells us that Agricola came north in 80CE and the neck of land between the Clyde and Forth,

> ... was now secured by garrisons, and the whole sweep of the country was safe in our hands. The enemy had been pushed into what was virtually another island.
>
> [Tacitus 23, pp.73–4]

The following year seems to have been spent in consolidating in particular the west coast of Britain and in the sixth year of his British campaign he began to concentrate on the lands to north of the Forth–Clyde line. Tacitus tells us that,

The war was pushed forward simultaneously by land and sea; and infantry, cavalry and marines, often meeting in the same camp, would mess and make merry together... The Britons, for their part, as was learned from prisoners, were stupefied by the appearance of the fleet. The mystery of their sea was divulged, their last refuge in defeat cut off.

[*Ibid* 25, p.75]

This shows the bias of Roman thinking. 'The mystery of their sea' is a strange way to describe waters that had been travelled over for millennia by a variety of cultures ever since the flourishing of the Megalith builders 3,000 years and more before the Romans found their way north. As in his later description of Calgacus, in terms which would not be out of place in the 18th century notion of the 'noble savage', Tacitus here shows us that we have to be particularly careful in using outside sources to try and understand our own culture. From the Roman point of view the illiterate, non-urban peoples of north Britain were not just barbarians – those living beyond the pale of acceptable civilisation – they were effectively savages, never mind the culture they came from.

He then goes on to make a remarkable statement:

Without provocation they attacked one of our forts, and inspired alarm by their challenging offensive.

[*Ibid* 25, p.75]

These offensive barbarians had the gall to attack the Romans invading their country! Battle ensues in which the Romans are victorious against the treacherous natives and he tells us that had there not been marshes and forests to cover the enemy's retreat the war would have ended there and then. He then tells of the battle of Mons Graupius. Before the battle Calgacus, the war leader of the Caledonians, is said to have inspired his troops with a speech worthy of any of the great Roman orators. Here we are seeing the process by which Agricola is elevated by being presented with a suitably brave and noble, if barbarian, opponent. The battle itself is said to have been fought by 30,000 natives and 11,000 Romans. Missiles were exchanged and then the Roman legions marched in step on to the enemy lines. The Caledonians had long swords and small shields which were more suitable for one-to-one combat and the Romans, fighting in unison using short stabbing swords from behind their large shields, soon routed them. The fact that the natives' swords had no thrusting point suggests their weapons were perhaps related to the later popular claymores or two-handed swords used for centuries in both Lowland and Highland Scotland. These large blades were swung two-handed rather than being used to thrust and parry. In the course of the Roman victory Tacitus tells us that around 10,000 of the natives fell and that the Roman casualties numbered 360. In the modern world we are well used to the inflated casualty figures put out by occupying forces in imperialist wars such as in Iraq and Afghanistan and I would suggest that Tacitus' numbers be treated similarly.

The location of this battle has been the cause of much discussion and nowadays the tendency is to see it as having taken place somewhere as far north as Aberdeenshire. While we know that the Romans under Agricola certainly did pass through Aberdeenshire and into Morayshire, there is no absolute reason to locate it there.

A recent article on the problem [Breeze, 2002] has suggested that the battle was fought near Bennachie, on the grounds that the term Graupius is possibly a Latin rendition of an indigenous P-Celtic term *crub* or *crip* meaning ridge. This is an attractive argument. However the location at Bennachie, while resting on the indisputable fact that Bennachie has a long ridge, is perhaps undermined by the name of the hill. The name Bennachie refers specifically to the nipple-shaped peak at the eastern end of the massif, known today as Mither Tap, but in earlier times as Mither Pap. This is a direct reference to the nipple or breast-shaped peak and as I have pointed out elsewhere [McHardy 2005, p.144ff; 2006, p.89] such sites seem to have been regarded as significant in the religion that pre-dated Christianity. Essentially I would suggest that such Paps were seen as being specifically related to an ancient mother goddess figure, and as such the Pap of Bennachie would have given the name of the massif. Whether another name referring specifically to the ridge ever existed is unproveable. An alternative location, following the same linguistic analysis, would be that the ridge in question is that of the Lomond Hills. Here we also have reference to breast-shaped hills – the Paps of Fife, East and West Lomond Hill – which can be seen from both Angus to the north and the Lothians to the south. I propose that the connecting ridge between these hills is at least as possible a location for a P-Celtic origin of the term *Graupius* as is Bennachie. Additionally

there are reports of considerable finds of Roman artefacts in the immediate area from the 19th century and earlier. Some of these are from
Merlsford, near Gateside on the north side of the Lomond Hills and a
mass burial was also found here which may support the idea of a local
battle. [Canmore URL].

Tacitus describes the behaviour of the enemy in the aftermath of the
battle thus:

> ... the Britons, when they saw our ranks steady and firm and the
> pursuit beginning again, simply turned and ran. They no longer
> kept any formation or any touch with one another, but deliber-
> ately broke into small groups to reach their far and trackless
> retreats.
>
> [*Ibid*, p.88]

The presentation of the victory at Mons Graupius as absolute is underlined by the fact that the enemy were seen to have scattered. They had
retreated back into the forests and mountains. Tacitus presents this as a
result of their defeat but another way of considering this is that they had
gone back to their scattered communities to regroup. It is a telling fact
that no other Roman source talks of a formal battle like Mons Graupius
in the north during the rest of the period of Roman occupation of southern Britain. Although there were later major outbreaks of warfare like
the Barbarian Conspiracy of 360, it would appear that the native warriors learned quickly that there was little use in fighting the disciplined
Roman fighting machine in set battles, particularly when their own
skills had been learned in the process of small-scale, fast-moving raids.
The scattering referred to can be seen as the Caledonians reverting back
to smaller-scale raiding groups after the battle. Something like modern
guerrilla warfare was clearly called for and would appear to have
become the norm for the next 300 years. This may well account for the
somewhat peculiar reference by Dio Cassio,

> They can endure hunger and cold and any kind of hardship; for
> they plunge into the swamps and exist there for many days with
> only their heads above water...
>
> [Dio 1927, p.293]

The description of the indigenous warriors up to their necks in swamps might well be referring to them taking advantage of the terrain to wait in ambush for small groups of Romans. Also the reference to their powers of endurance is something which is echoed in references to the warriors of late Highland society.

Archaeology has shown that probably following Agricola's march into battle at Mons Graupius, an attempt had been made to set up a new frontier deep into what we now know as Scotland. This comprised the Gask Ridge, a series of fortlets or signal stations, which were constructed along the ridge of land running from the river Teith at Doune, near Stirling, to what is now the city of Perth on the Tay, linked to a series of larger fortifications at what are known as the Glen Forts of Fendoch, Dalginross, Bochastle, Malling and Drumquassle.

This border seems to have been abandoned by 86CE [Woolliscroft URL]. The forts ran at intervals along the line between Teith and the Tay. While this border was not a continuous wall, it can be seen as Rome's earliest attempt at a fortified land frontier in northern Britain and it is possible that it was part of Agricola's attempt to subdue the north. The fortifications cover the boundary between Scotland's mountainous Highland zone in Perthshire and Angus and the less mountainous Lowland areas to the south, and there have been suggestions that the intent was to provide protection for the more fertile land to the south and east of this line. However this suggestion would depend on there having been an area of controlled Roman occupation of those areas and that they were being cultivated to an extent that appears unlikely given what the Roman sources tell us of the life-style of the inhabitants. Archaeology may yet find evidence of large-scale farming in southern Scotland during this period but as yet there is none. It was however part of Roman imperial policy to use forward planning and it may well have been their intent to develop southern Scotland as much of eastern and central England undoubtedly was. If so, they simply never got the chance.

The precise relationship with the smaller constructions of the Gask Ridge and the Glen Forts is as yet unclear but together they suggest the Roman intention was to cover the major glen or valley mouths in the Highland line to prevent large numbers of natives pouring south. However given the nature of the raiding tradition of the natives, they were much more likely to have moved in small fast-moving groups which would have no need to restrict themselves to the major glens. This sums up the Romans' quandary. Their conquest of Europe had relied on the organised and regular disposition of highly disciplined legions, numbering thousands of men each, and here they were in a terrain in which the deployment of such troops was highly problematic. On the other hand the small groups of native warriors, trained in raiding within the environment, would have no problems in using their own military skills in any situation where the Romans were exposed. The hit-and-run tactics of modern guerrilla warfare serves well as a model for attempting to understand how the indigenous peoples surely resisted the might of the Roman armies.

There is no evidence to suggest that the Roman forts of this early period were in continued occupation till the next major incursion. Extensive excavation of a series of Roman sites has made it clear that in the period soon after the battle of Mons Graupius the Romans retreated south. Their supposed crushing victory and the subsequent flight of the Caledonians 'to their far and trackless retreats' did not apparently lead to Roman control of the country. If Agricola had defeated the indigenous peoples and established control over their lands Tacitus would certainly have mentioned it. The fact that subsequent invasions took place shows that it was Imperial policy to try and conquer the entire island and the conclusion must be that it was simply not a viable proposition at this time. A hint of the reason for this is made by Tacitus when he tells us 'when they reached the woods, they rallied and profited by their local knowledge to ambush the rash pursuers.' [*Ibid.*] This would appear to underline the native use of the rugged and heavily wooded terrain and given that we hear of no further pitched battles other than at the Roman walls over the next three centuries, it would appear that the native warriors quickly realised that their own style of battle, based on the swift and adaptable tactics of inter-tribal raiding were the most effective means of combating the organised regiments of the Imperial army for whom such terrain would always prove difficult.

Tacitus tells us that Agricola was recalled to Rome by the Emperor Domitian having 'handed over a province peaceful and secure to his successor.' [1948, 40 p.91.] We can be sure that he did not mean all of Britain but could he be referring to all the country up to the line of the Gask forts? Archaeology tells us that these forts were abandoned around this time so it seems as if his reference to a 'secure province' referred to what is now England and Wales. I suggest he meant that having defeated the massed ranks of the tribes to the north, the southern half of Britain was now secure. Certainly within a few years of Mons Graupius the Romans had retreated from Scotland and though the immediate reason was apparently the need for the legions elsewhere, it is notable that at no later date is there any evidence of there having been any significant attempt at creating a border north of the Gask ridge. Effectively, in their first incursion into the country they got as far north as they ever would. The north remained free of Roman domination and the tribes there could continue to live as they always had done. It seems transparently obvious that they continued to raid to the south, necessitating the creation and continued manning of Hadrian's Wall, and leading in time to another attempt to move the frontier north. The Roman failure suggests that whatever specific form the society of the Pictish tribes took, it had the capacity for the divergent tribes to unite in times of stress and this would likely be a direct development of what had gone before. It must have preserved a continuity with the culture of the far past in ways that the Romanised areas to the south lost forever.

Hadrian's Wall

It was 60 years before the Romans again mounted a serious effort to conquer the northern tribes, but in the meantime defences against the northern tribes had to be strengthened. In 122CE, five years after becoming Emperor, Hadrian ordered the construction of a great wall between modern Wallsend in the east and Bowness on the Solway Firth in the west. This followed him visiting Britian and becoming aware of the ongoing problems with the indigenous tribes to the north. The construction of Hadrian's Wall was clearly intended to stop any incursions from the Pictish and Scottish tribes and its construction in stone can be construed as it being created as, if not a permanent border, then at least a serious attempt at preventing incursions and defending the increasingly Romanised areas to the south. Imperial control of the territory of even warlike tribes such as the Brigantes in northern England meant that they perceived the area south of the wall to be worth defending. It was now obviously part of the Roman Empire while the lands to the north, just as obviously, were not. The construction of the wall, with a great ditch and regular forts along its length, suggests that raids from the north were an ongoing problem. Although the construction of this great edifice was in itself an act of Imperial grandeur it was also practical. Its very construction tells us that the tribal peoples to the north were still unconquered and were perceived of as a permanent danger to the now Roman lands to the south. Smyth makes a very interesting point as to the Roman presence in northern Britain when he tells us

> ... those isolated forts along the sprawling frontier of Roman Britain most certainly housed press-gangs and slave raiders who preyed on the natives in order to supplement the unscrupulous procurators' income and to maintain the supply of forced labour in the iron industries... in Northumberland, and in numerous other industries further south. Taking the northern British tribes as a whole it is hard to see what incentives they had to collaborate with Rome.
>
> [Smyth 1984, p.15]

Whether or not we give credence to the speech attributed to Calgacus by Tacitus before the battle of Mons Graupius and the claim that the assembled tribal warriors were 'the last of the Free', the northern tribes had every reason to resist Rome and the very construction of Hadrian's Wall suggests that they were effective in doing so. They had seen how their cousins, like the tribes of the Iceni and the Brigantes to the south, had been conquered and enslaved by the Romans, and this can only have stiffened their resolve to resist the invaders. The analogy with the later Highland tribes provides a relevant comparison with this attitude as it was only in the 18th century that centralised government control was imposed on them. At the core of these warrior societies was a refusal to be dominated. Their resistance to government control reminds us that government, by its very nature, is not necessarily benificent. We should also remember that the loyalty of the tribal warriors was to their own kin, the tribe, and that modern ideas of the nation state, or of a cultural homogeneity defined by language are anachronistic in analysing the period. This refusal to be dominated was to become a central aspect of the development of what became Scotland, as the threat of invasion, particularly from England, was to remain virtually constant till the end of the 17th century.

The Northern Wall

In or around 143CE the Roman Governor of Britain, Antoninus Pius, built a wall across the narrowest part of Scotland between the Forth and Clyde rivers. This had a total of 10 or 11 forts along its 37 mile length compared with 16 forts on the 73 miles of Hadrian's Wall. Unlike Hadrian's Wall, which was primarily built of stone, the northern wall was constructed for most of its length from turf with a section of earthen wall faced with clay. There was a ditch about 20 feet north of the wall, 40 feet wide and about 12 feet deep. The forts attached to the wall were likewise mainly built of turf. It has been assumed by many commentators that the area between the walls was to some degree or other under the total control of Rome. Given the short lifetime of the northern wall and the subsequent retreat to Hadrian's Wall c.165AD, this can hardly be the case. Hadrian's Wall stood against incursion from the north for around 280 years while the Antonine Wall, according to the latest archaeology, stood for less than 30. Given the greater frequency of major fortifications along the northern wall we are surely justified in considering whether this might have been because the necessity was to defend against the possibility of attack from both the north and the south of the wall. As noted above, the currently accepted date for the destruction of the northern wall is in the 160s and it is also notable that several of the forts along its length have been shown to have been extensively damaged c.155CE and abandoned for a while, most probably due to the revolt of the tribe of the Brigantes in northern England. If this could happen within the area supposedly defended by Hadrian's Wall and within the ambit of the Roman Empire, it raises the question of whether the tribes to the north, the Votadini, Selgovae, Novantae and Damnonii had actually been conquered. Tacitus claimed a series of victories against the tribes, but Agricola had retreated, giving those tribes time to regroup. Also, considering the tactics of the native peoples, the assumption that being defeated in battle by the Romans meant they had been conquered is not one that can be substantiated. The construction of Hadrian's Wall shows the probability that these tribes, though having suffered defeats, were not cowed, far less controlled. In the light of this the pushing north of the frontier by Antonius Pius may best be understood as an attempt at preventing further raiding and does not imply actual conquest. In fact that the northern wall was built of earth and turf shows it to be a much more temporary structure than Hadrian's Wall. There may also have been some economic reasoning behind its construction, as the line it takes between the Clyde and Forth rivers appears to have been a major trading route.

It is likely that the wall was supplied by sea through the Forth and/or the Clyde, for though we know that the native peoples had a sailing tradition dating back to at least Megalithic times, there is no evidence for any shipping that could have viably attacked the large Roman galleys of the period, particularly if they arrived as a fleet. Much of the land between the walls was heavily forested, other areas boggy, and there is no evidence to suggest that people there were any different from the tribes to the north. Roman occupation was mainly limited to forts along the supply lines from the south running through the Southern Uplands, one through modern Moffat and Dumfries and the other through to Melrose and the great fort on the Eildon Hills, called Trimontium by the Romans, and south to Hadrian's Wall. Settlements outside those of the wall like Cramond and Inveresk could well have been supplied by sea and cannot be taken as clear evidence of anything more than localised Roman control. After little more than 20 years the Antonine Wall was abandoned and the Roman frontier retreated to Hadrian's Wall.

In the past it has been argued that at least some of the tribes between the two walls must have been clients of the Romans and that some of them may even have been active in helping to defend the frontier on behalf of the Romans. However there is no real evidence for this and the length of time the northern wall lasted would argue against this. If the tribes of southern Scotland, whom as it has been noted were included by the Romans in the generic terms Caledonian and Pict, had been linked to the Roman Empire we would expect there to be some archaeological evidence from the extensive investigation of Roman sites in Scotland. There is however nothing to support this idea and the famous hoard of Roman silver and coins from Traprain Law dates from the end of the fourth century and seems more likely to have been the spoils of raiding rather than any kind of gift or payment. The silver found there was crushed, ready to be melted down and re-used, which argues as much for booty as gifts. Also, as Smyth points out [1984, p.15] there is no evidence from the Traprain Law site to suggest any significant Roman influence on local society. He also makes the point that the idea that Roman influence on the northern tribes can be inferred from the Latinized forms of personal names appearing in later genealogies is more likely to be due to the influence of Christianity or, he suggests, could have arisen from a wish to emulate the powerful Romans. This I suggest is less likely than the simple fact of literacy. The genealogies that survived in Welsh regarding the *Gwr Y Gogledd*, the Men of the North, were not written down till centuries after the period but the significant point is perhaps not their lack of contemporaeity. The important factor here is surely that they were written down and as with all surviving early British literature the process of writing itself was influenced by the Classical, and Christian, thinking of those who were doing the recording. Literature arrived with the Romans and developed under the influence of Christianity, a religion that was heavily influenced by Classical scholarship. The literary and apparently Classically-influenced form of the names is not necessarily what the names were on the lips of the indigenous people. A further point Smyth makes [*Ibid*, p.40] is that Roman artefacts, including the hoard from Traprain Law, an important site of the Votadini tribe, are much thinner on the ground in Scotland than similar finds from East Prussia, an area that the Romans never visited. The East Prussian finds were clearly the result of either trade or plunder and they can in no way be seen as evidence of direct Roman control over the local people. The idea that a more limited range of finds can be construed in Scotland as evidence of the southern tribes being clients of Rome would appear to be more to do with the dominant role of Classical studies in Scottish education within the British state than anything else. While this mindset can be seen as a natural by-product of British Imperialism, which was to some extent philosophically modelled on the Romans, it certainly does not help in trying to gain a clearer picture of the past in what is now Scotland.

As we shall see later the descendants of the Votadini, under their indigenous name the Gododdin, seem to still have been a warrior raiding society at the close of the seventh century, despite having had some proximity to the Romans over several centuries and also having become Christianised in the intervening years. They should therefore be seen as one component part of ongoing tribal Scotland in the period up to the seventh century, and certainly from the perspective of the Romans as essentially Pictish.

In or around 184CE when Commodus was the general in charge of Britain, the Picts came across Hadrian's Wall and according to Dio, killed a general and his troops [1927, p.87] and were driven back. In 193CE

Clodius Albinus took over as governor of Britain. Hearing that the Emperor Pertinax had been murdered, Clodus decided to try and become Emperor himself. Far off in Pannonia, modern Hungary, Septimus Severus was declared Emperor by the troops he commanded. He offered Albinus the title of Caesar and to nominate him as his heir. This was accepted and as Severus consolidated his grip on the Roman Empire, Clodius appeared to remain loyal. However Severus soon learned he was plotting to become Emperor himself [Dio 1927, p.203]. In 196 he had himself declared Emperor in Britain and headed to Gaul at the head of his own troops. After a bloody campaign they met in a seesaw battle at Lyon which Severus eventually won. It was at this time that the Picts appear to have taken advantage of Clodius removing his troops in the north, or at least severely reducing their numbers, and both Hadrian's Wall and several forts in the Pennines were badly damaged, quite possibly with the assistance of local tribes like the Brigantes who were dissatisfied with Roman rule. We cannot be sure exactly what happened but the incursion showed that the northern tribes were ready to maraud south whenever the opportunity presented itself. This prompted Severus to come to Britain to try and re-establish control. After repairing the Pennine forts and Hadrian's Wall, he decided that attack was the best method of defence and proceeded to invade the northern half of Britain, to try and finally conquer the northern tribes.

So in the year 208CE Severus came north with an army. It seems fair to assume that the Romans had failed to secure the lands between Hadrian's Wall and the Forth–Clyde axis other than during the 20 year period of the Antonine Wall. This is not to say that there was no Roman presence in southern Scotland at the time. The power of the Roman navy was such that Roman forts such as at Cramond on the Forth and Carpow on the Tay could have survived for a time, being supplied by sea. However again this would mean little other than localised control. The Roman army on the march would always be a daunting power but once it had passed we can posit that local people would revert to their normal way of life. The influence of Rome undoubtedly over time gave impetus towards the development of a money economy but there is no evidence that the indigenous people of the north lived in anything other than a barter economy at this period and though there would have been some trading between the Romans and the natives, it does not seem to have been extensive enough to alter the fundamental realities of everyday existence for the natives. And there is no reason to think that raiding did not continue. Whether or not the Romans actually paid the tribes to stop raiding must remain moot.

Again the similarity with late Highland society is perhaps informative. While they may have been looked on by their Lowland neighbours as cattle thieves, the Highland clansmen, as has been noted, believed that the 'lifting' of cattle was proper behaviour for a Highland gentleman, and to all intents and purposes every member of the clan saw himself as such. Also given the tribal nature of indigenous society the Romans would have had to bribe all the tribes abutting the wall to have had much effect. Bribing one tribe would not affect the others.

In the late 80sCE the Romans retreated south and even if there were external reasons for withdrawing the legions in the north it is clear that, as happened when Albinus withdrew his troops, the Picts took the opportunity to raid south again. The attempt to conquer the tribal peoples of northern Britain, whether we call them the Picts or Caledonians, had been a failure.

Dio tells us of Britain,

Its length is 951 miles, its greatest breadth 308, and its least 40. Of this territory we hold a little less than one half.

Severus, accordingly, desiring to subjugate the whole of it, invaded Caledonia. But as he advanced through the country he experienced countless hardships in cutting down the forests, levelling the heights, filling up the swamps, and bridging the rivers; but he fought no battle and beheld no enemy in battle array. The enemy purposefully put sheep and cattle in front of the soldiers for them to seize, in order that they might be lured on still further until they were worn out; for in fact the water caused great suffering to the Romans, and when they became scattered, they would be attacked. Then unable to walk, they would be slain by their own men, in order to avoid capture, so that a full 50,000 of them died. But Severus did not desist until he approached the extremity of the island... he returned to the friendly proportion, after he had forced the Britons to come to terms, on the condition that they should abandon a large part of their territory.

[1927, pp.266–7]

Before setting out on this campaign Severus had repaired Hadrian's Wall and from the context it appears clear that Caledonia here means all the land to the north of the wall. The reference to 'no battle' and the attacks on the Roman forces are a clear indication of small-scale guerrilla tactics on behalf of the Picts, though the figure of 50,000 dead seems exaggerated. Herodian tells us that,

> After the army had crossed the rivers and fortifications which marked the borders of the empire, there were frequent clashes and light skirmishes in which the barbarians were put to flight. The enemy found it easy to escape and hide in the woods and marshes because they were familiar with the terrain; but the same conditions all hampered the Romans and made the war considerably longer drawn out...
>
> [Herodian 1949, p.365]

Again this sounds not as if the Picts are being 'put to flight' so much as employing hit-and-run tactics. However, without any decisive battle how should we accept that Severus forced the 'Britons' to come to terms? This is propagandistic and, like the statement of him approaching the extremity of the island in Dio Cassio, when archaeology suggests he got no further than Morayshire, suggests that effectively Dio is putting Severus' actions in the best possible light. Without a major battle Severus could not defeat the tribes and his retreat to the 'friendly portion' of Britain says it all. Yet again the Romans had invaded Scotland with a large army and yet again they retreated back south. In recounting how Severus' son Antoninus tried to assassinate his own father Dio tells us that they were riding forward to meet the Caledonians to discuss a truce [*Ibid*, p.269]. Whether or not there was a truce as such, this is difficult to square with Severus forcing the natives to come to terms. Given the nature of their tactics, without further details it is difficult to give much credence to the idea that the indigenous people ceded half of their territory to Rome, particularly as the army retreated back behind Hadrian's Wall. Dio then tells us that after all this the inhabitants of the island 'revolted'. He tells us of Severus's reaction:

> ... he summoned the soldiers and ordered them to invade the rebels' country, killing everybody they met; and he quoted these

words; [from Homer] 'Let no one escape sheer destruction, and the might of our hands, not even the babe in the womb of the mother, if it be male; let it nevertheless not escape sheer destruction.'

[*Ibid*, p.271]

This is a clear example of just how brutal Roman Imperial policy often was though it should be said that Severus did have a particular reputation for ruthlessness. The situation however is somewhat unclear for he goes on:

When this had been done, and the Caledonians had joined the revolt of the Maetae, he began preparing to make war upon them in person.

[*Ibid*]

It was at this period that the illness from which Severus had been suffering killed him, and Dio says, 'not without some help, they say from Antoninus.' [*Ibid*.] This is a further example of the brutality that lay at the heart of Imperial politics and reminds us that the idea of Rome as a civilising force is somewhat trite. However the point is surely that we see the Caledonians and Maetae again uniting against Rome. The simplest reading of this is surely that the genocidal activities ordered by Severus took place among the Maetae, the tribe(s) closest to Hadrian's Wall, and that their neighbours to the north came to their assistance. Severus' brutality instead of cowing the natives merely served to unite them against the Empire. However, the ability of the different tribes to combine against the Romans, as shown in the account of Mons Graupius, does not in itself suggest any level of societal cohesion beyond that of the tribe. Once his father was dead Antoninus, according to Dio, slaughtered his father's household, gave promises and gifts to the commanders of the army and 'came to terms with the barbarians, granting them peace in return for guarantees [*Ibid*, p.367]. This sounds like the standard practice of taking hostages but we have no absolute proof of this and Antoninus' next action is telling. He left the north to meet with his brother Geta to arrange ruling Rome together. Yet again we find that the Roman sources tell us that there are other reasons for the Romans leaving without finally conquering the north of Britain. Herodian's final word on this is worth considering. He tells us that the brothers and their mother headed for the Continent,

Associating themselves with the army as though they were returning as conquerors of Britain, they crossed the ocean and landed on the opposite shore of Gaul...

[*Ibid*, p.369]

It is notable that he does not say conquerors of Caledonia, or of the Caledonians, but of Britain. The suggestion is that they were effectively trying to cover themselves in their father's glory, but in the light of the fact that Hadrian's Wall remained as the northern frontier we are entitled to think that the Picts had once again repulsed an invading Roman army. The massive 30 acre fortress at Carpow on the river Tay near Abernethy which was not started until 208AD towards the end of this campaign seems to have been left as an outpost and was probably supplied by ships sailing up the Tay, but it too was abandoned by 215CE. Its construction of stone shows that Severus had intended it as a permanent garrison. No matter what control the Romans may have had over parts of Scotland in this campaign it did not last.

CHAPTER THREE

Standoff and survival

BY THE EARLY PART of the third century the natives had once again forced the Romans back behind Hadrian's Wall. It appears likely that Severus supplied his army from the sea – thus avoiding the necessity of long and vulnerable supply lines from the south – and this could mean that he was intent on a punitive campaign against the native tribes rather than attempting to conquer the whole of Scotland, rather than setting up staged bases along the line of their invasion, around which they could take absolute control of the countryside as they did in England. His eventual successor, his son Caracalla, did not follow this up and the frontier drew back south to Hadrian's Wall. This may well have been a result of the casualties mentioned by Dio Cassius, even if the figure of 50,000 is an exaggeration.

The Romans had once more come and gone. Dio's report tells us something of the life of the indigenous people, referring to the Maetae and the Caledonii he tells us:

Both tribes inhabit... wild and waterless mountains and desolate and swampy plains, and possess neither walls, cities, nor tilled fields, but live on their flocks, wild game, and certain fruits; for they do not touch the fish which are found there in immense and inexhaustible quantities. They dwell in tents, naked and unshod, possess their women in common, and in common rear all the offspring. Their form of rule is democratic for the most part, and they are very fond of plundering; consequently they choose their best men as rulers. They go into battle in chariots, and have small swift horses; there are also foot-soldiers, very swift in running and very firm in standing their ground. For arms they have a shield and a short spear, with a bronze apple attached to the end of the spear-shaft, so that when it is shaken it may clash and terrify the enemy; and they also have daggers... in the forests they support themselves upon bark and roots, and for all emergencies they prepare a certain kind of food, the eating of a small portion of which, the size of a bean, prevents them from feeling either hunger or thirst.

[*Ibid*, pp.264–5]

This description from the pen of Dio Cassius, writing thousands of miles away in Rome, is not an eye-witness account. However there can be little doubt that his description was gleaned from those who had actually served in Scotland. And, as we have nothing else to tell us of Scotland in this period we are forced to rely on such testimony, and while remaining careful of second or even third hand accounts, careful analysis of such material can help us gain a picture of what the Romans saw.

The specific description of these northern warriors is remarkable in that we can still see an indigenous version of it on the symbol stone at Collessie in Fife. The figure on the stone is carrying a ball-ended spear as described by Dio and a small shield. He also appears to be wearing little other than a cloak which is reminiscent of that other Roman source Herodian saying that the natives 'do not wear clothes' [1949, p.359]. There is also a carved pillar stone in the Museum of Scotland from Bridgeness on the Forth, originally part of the Antonine Wall, depicting three naked natives cowering below a Roman cavalryman. The depiction on the Collessie stone is itself remarkable in that modern received opinion regarding the Pictish symbol stones sees them as being no earlier than the sixth century, 300 years after Dio described such a man. There are also similarities with other fragmented stones which also have single warriors on them at Rhynie in Aberdeenshire and Balblair in Angus. Thus either the Picts carried on the military traditions of their ancestors in a specific fashion till long after the Roman period, or the carving on the Collessie stone is in fact much older than is generally supposed. By the time we have other representations of fighting Picts, such as at Aberlemno or on the Dull stone, several more centuries have passed and it is clear that the dress and weaponry of the indigenous warriors had changed substantially from the representation on the Collessie stone. However as yet we have no detailed archaeological investigation of sufficient numbers of Pictish sites from the early centuries of the First Millennium to clarify the situation, so we are entitled to pose the question – is the Collessie stone, and likewise are some other Class 1 stones, which have simple pecked out carvings on naturally shaped stone – considerably older than is generally supposed? This carving would surely have to have been executed while the use of the weaponry depicted on it was still extant. To this extent it is like the Aberlemno stone generally accepted as depicting the battle of Dunnichen in 685CE. After all we have a written source and a matching carving, so it makes more sense to see them as contemporaneous than anything else. Therefore can we take it that Collessie man appears to be no later than the second or third century? Short of the archaeological discovery of dateable artefacts such as a ball-ended spear in conjunction with a symbol stone, we cannot be absolutely sure but the match between the description and the written report is relatively exact.

As has been noted above, carving on stone had been known in Scotland for millennia before the Romans arrived, with deer occurring alongside cup-and-ring markings, generally accepted to be no later than 1500BCE. In the light of this we must consider the possibility that the earliest stones, Class I by the classification suggested by Romilly Allen, [1993, Part II pp.3–4] are much earlier than has generally been accepted till now, the standard approach seeing them as being carved from the sixth to the tenth centuries. The classification describes Class II as upright dressed stone cross-slabs with Pictish symbols and Christian iconography on opposite sides, and Class III are those which do not fall into either of the previous two categories, can be upright or recumbent and do not have Pictish symbols thereon. While Class I have simple incised carving, the other two classes are usually carved in relief, though may include some incision. While it is clear that the Picts did not need the Romans, or anyone else, to show them how to carve on stone, the later stones, Classes II and III, do seem to have developed as a result of external, specifically Christian influence. As it is now clear that the Antonine Wall was no longer extant after the mid 160s, any direct influence from Roman stone working techniques would be more likely to occur in the areas closest to Hadrian's Wall, while the vast majority of First Millennium sculpture in Scotland comes from further north. However we have little to rely on that is securely dated to the first few centuries of the First Millennium other than Roman sources and we must consider what these actually tell us about the Picts.

The geography which Dio clearly finds oppressive – the modern idea of Scotland's landscape as beautiful does not pre-date the early 19th century – was of course the normal environment for the indigenous peoples and the reference to the lack of walls and cities underlines the scattered, small-scale nature of local communities which survived in the Scottish

Lowlands in the fermtoun tradition till the dawn of modern agriculture, and in the Highland tradition of clachans into even more recent times. The reference to no tilled fields is demonstrably wrong as we have archaeological evidence for limited arable farming from as early as the Second Millennium BCE [Calder 1955–6, p.375] The reference to flocks suggests a reliance on a basically pastoral economy which is also something that survived into modern times in many parts of Scotland and specifically in Highland areas. The use of the word democratic is somewhat anachronistic but may refer to the fact that tribalism is generally egalitarian in that status does not suggest political power over others, and the fact that there is often some element of election in the choice of chiefs. Solinus, in the English translation of Arthur Golding, refers to the 'kings' among the indigenous peoples thus:

> The king hath nothing of hys own, but taketh from every mans. Hee is bound to equitie by certaine lawes: and lest he may start from right through covetousness, he learneth justice by povertie, as who may have nothing proper or peculiar to himselfe, but is found at the charges of the Realme. Hee is not suffered to have anie woman to himselfe, but whomsoever he hath minde unto, he borroweth for a tyme, and so others by turnes. Whereby it comes to passe that he hath neither desire nor hope of issue.
>
> [Solinus 1999, 22, pp.11–17]

As with other references to the society of the Picts there is this notion that the women are held in common in some way. This is surely no more than an outsider's confused view of a tribal society in which the centrality of the kin-group was misunderstood. We will look more closely at the possibility of some sort of matrilineal structure later. What is clear from the Roman sources throughout the Imperial presence in the British Isles is that the peoples of the north, the Picts on this reading, continued to function as tribal societies and were a constant thorn in the flesh of the Empire.

There are other aspects of Dio's description which are particularly interesting. The reference to a 'certain kind of food' would appear to mean the tubers which grow on the roots of the bitter vetch plant. These tubers, bean-sized as Dio says, were collected by Highland families as late as the 18th century. Dr Brian Moffat of SHARP, the organisation in charge of the investigation of the medieval hospital at Soutra, south of Edinburgh, has identified this as the Heath Pea or Karemyle, tubers that grow on the roots of the bitter vetch plant. Dr Moffat has shown [2000 *passim*] that this plant was known and utilised in Scotland into the 18th century. He is also quite sure that this 'certain kind of food' was in widespread use throughout northern Europe in the past. It was harvested and dried as a stand-by in case of shortages of food, a threat that is always present in communities that rely on self-sufficient food production. The reference to the endurance of the warriors and their skill at living off the land is again redolent of late descriptions of Highland warriors whose endurance was legendary. The specific reference to standing in swamps with only their heads showing can be interpreted as one of the tactics they used to ambush the Romans when they 'became scattered'. The desolation that the Romans perceived was home to these warriors and their families and it is a classic aspect of guerrilla warfare that indigenous peoples are at home within their environment, physical and social, whereas invaders are not.

We have little evidence as yet for what was going on in Scotland in the century following the Roman retreat in 211CE. As there are few even Roman records referring to particular involvement with the northern tribes from this period it is, I suggest, safe to assume that the situation that required the continued maintenance of the Wall against incursions from the north continued. Herodian, when he refers to the natives as 'warlike and savage' [1929, p.359], appears to be presenting what was the dominant Roman attitude to the tribal peoples of northern Britain. From the point of view of those peoples themselves we can surmise that they never lost sight of the fact that the Romans were out to conquer and effectively enslave them so the continuance of hostilities made absolute sense to them. By the beginning of the fourth century however yet another attempt at conquest appears to have been made.

Before this we have a significant date regarding the Picts. This was 297CE, the year in which an anonymous writer composed a panegyric to the Emperor Constantius. Referring to Julius Caesar's invasion of Britain *c.*55BCE the writer refers to the Britons as:

A nation which was then primitive, and accustomed to fight, still half-naked, only with Picts and Hiberni, easily succumbed to

Roman arms, almost to the point that Caesar should have boasted about this one thing on that expedition; that he had sailed across the Ocean.

[Nixon 1994, pp.126–7]

Panegyrics were literary essays of praise, usually to Emperors, and we can assume that the author was highly educated and thus aware of common historical knowledge. It is noticeable that the reference to the Irish tribes is Hiberni not Scots, which in the light of Campbell's suggestion that the Scots did not originate in Ireland is significant [Campbell 2000, p.222]. The statement also suggests that the author saw the Picts as a historic people at the time he is referring to i.e. he believed that the inhabitants of the northern part of the British Isles in his own time were the same people as in Caesar's time. There is a certain irony in this statement having long been the basis for suggesting that the term Pictish should only, properly, be used from this date onwards on the basis that this is the first recorded use of the term. The reference clearly shows that the writer saw the Picts as one of the indigenous British peoples who were around in the time of Julius Caesar. The writer is also scoffing at the pathetic Picts, who in fact continued to hold out against Roman conquest till their Empire began to collapse and they withdrew from Britain entirely.

Within 10 years of this however we have some evidence for yet another invasion to the north. Constantius came to Britain in the early years of the fourth century to quell a rebellion started by the Roman Commander Carausis and carried on by Allectus whom it seems had killed Carausis. A reference in the *Panegyric of Constantine* mentions 'the forests and swamps of the Caledonians and the other Picts' [Nixon 1994, p.227] and a passage in the work known as the *Anonymous Valesianus* says that Constantius died at York 'after winning a victory over the Picts' [Ammianus 1909, III, p.511].

Frere in *Britannia* suggests that the Picts had taken advantage of Allectus removing troops from Hadrian's Wall to help in his struggle with Constantius, to conduct a series of raids over the Wall [Frere 1987, p.332]. He goes on to make the point that

There is no doubt that the great majority, if not all, of the forts of northern Britain were extensively rebuilt about the beginning of the fourth century.

[Frere 1987, p.334]

As previously noted there has long been a tendency for historians in Britain to make assumptions about the Romans. They were after all the intellectual model for the creation of the British Empire, were in England for 400 years and have often been presented as essentially beneficent. The experience of the Picts at the hands of Severus and the ongoing struggles with the northern tribes shows that they must have had a different concept of Roman power. They were more than aware of the brutality of the Roman war machine. Historians of the Roman Empire on the other hand have all too often been blinded by the power and majesty of the Empire itself and this bias is often quite explicit. Frere tells us of Constantius:

> The details of the campaign are unknown, but the words of the Panegyrist make it plain that the far north of Scotland was reached. It seems probable that Severus' amphibious tactics were employed. Pottery of appropriate date has been discovered at Cramond and Carpow, where contact could be made with the sea, but otherwise there are no known archaeological traces of the expedition. Before midsummer a brilliant victory had been won, and Constantius returned to York where on 25 July he died.
>
> [Frere 1978, p.335]

What the Panegyrist actually says is that Constantius 'gazed upon the Ocean' [Nixon, p.227], presumably meaning that he got to the far north of Scotland and looked out over the Atlantic Ocean. There is no archaeological evidence to support this nor is there any specific mention of a 'brilliant victory' – it is merely assumed that there must have been one. It is always bad historical practice to accept one source uncritically but to add to it is something much worse. The supporting reference, from *Anonymous Valesianus* is 'Constantius, after winning a victory over the Picts died at York.' [Ammianus III 1939, p.511]. So there are two references one of which directly claims a victory, so it must have been a brilliant one! From the Pictish point of view Constantius, whether or not he had managed to lure the tribes into a pitched battle and defeat them, did as all the other Romans before him had done, he left. We must always treat the Roman sources critically as they are quite obviously propagandistic in their intent but it is regrettable that latter day historians of Roman occupation continue to be so smitten with the glamour of the Empire.

On Constantius' death his son Constantine who was in attendance at York was declared Emperor. Before leaving he oversaw upgrading of the roads in England which Frere [*Ibid*, p.336] sees as a continuation of his father's policy of rebuilding and strengthening forts. The roads were important for both communications and the rapid deployment of troops. However it is noticeable that he did not follow up his father's incursion to the north. Yet again we see a Roman invasion, claims of great victory then apparently no attempt at consolidation which would have had to require substantial fort building to sustain an occupation. From the point of view of the Picts it must have seemed that the Romans were intent on little more than punitive attacks, presumably provoked by regular if not constant raiding on and beyond Hadrian's Wall. That there may have been some sort of Roman presence on a semi-permanent basis directly to the north of the wall has not been shown by archaeology but such a presence would have been open to almost permanent attack from the indigenous tribes of the immediate area, the Votadini, Selgovae, Damnonii and perhaps even the Novantae from further west.

Frere [*Ibid*, p.336–7] suggests that another Emperor, Constans I, after defeating his brother Constantine came to Britain because of a crisis in the north and suggests not only that he mounted a campaign against the Picts, but that he 'subdued' them. He tells, in referring to the year 360CE,

> ... the Scots and Picts of central Scotland broke the terms which had been imposed upon them, presumably by Constans, and began to lay waste the regions near the frontier.
>
> [*Ibid*, p.339]

Details of terms being imposed upon the Scots and Picts are, as far as I am aware, non-existent. Frere also mentions here that the Scots were 'still based in Ireland', but refers to them attacking the Romans alongside the Picts.

I have suggested that the tribes of southern Scotland, the Votadini, Selgovae, Damnonii and Novantae were included in the generic term Picts as used by the Romans. It is in the 360s that we first begin to hear of the Scots. For centuries it has been accepted that the Scots came into Argyll from Ulster around the year 500CE. This idea is based on documents which have been shown by to have been written no earlier than the 10th century. Campbell challenges this interpretation when he tells us:

In the Annals of Tighernach, an entry for around AD500 reads, '*Feargus mor mac earca cum gente dalriada partem britania tenuit et ibi mortus est*' — 'Fergus Mor mac Erc, with the nation of Dal Riada, took (or held) part of Britain, and died there'. This clear statement of invasion and colonisation is, however, not a contemporary record, as is shown by the form of the Irish words. *Dalriada*, *Feargus* and *Earca* are Middle Irish forms where one would expect the Old Irish *Dalriata*, *Fergus* and *Erca*. These spellings show that the entry could not have been written before the 10th century. It has been strongly argued that this entry, which is the earliest independent record of Fergus, is one of a series of insertions in the Annals derived from a 10th-century *Chronicle of Clonmacnoise* (Dumville 1993:187: Grabowski & Dumville 1984) and cannot be taken as independent evidence of colonisation.

The other main source is the *Senchus Fer nAlban* (History of the Men of Scotland). This very important document is a social survey and genealogy of the kings of *Dal Riata*, believed to have been originally written in the later seventh century and modified in the 10th century (Bannerman 1974). Even accepting the sup-posedly 10th-century version of the text uncritically, it does not refer to settlement but is a genealogical statement of the origins of the Scottish kings: '*Erc, moreover had twelve sons, six of them took possession of Alba.*' (Bannerman 1974: 47), and there follows a genealogy of the Dalriadan kings from Fergus Mor to the mid seventh century. It is important to note that nowhere is a mass movement of peoples mentioned, it is purely an aristocratic, and specifically royal, takeover of Scotland. However, this account also cannot be a contemporary record, and can be shown to be part of the 10th century or later rewriting of the original text (Bannerman 1974, 130–32), as *Alba* was not used as a term for Scotland before the 10th century.

[2001, p.288]

Having noted the lack of archaeological evidence and the equal lack of linguistic support for the idea of either a large-scale invasion or a purely dynastic takeover he goes on,

I suggest that the people inhabiting Argyll maintained a regional identity from at least the Iron Age through to the medieval period and that throughout this period they were Gaelic speakers. In this maritime province, sea communications dominated, and allowed a shared archaic language to be maintained, isolated from linguistic developments which were taking place in the areas of Britain to the east of the Highland massif in the Late Roman period.

[*Ibid*, p.291]

From this it would appear that the Scots first mentioned in the late fourth century are not the same as the Hiberni, mentioned in the *Panegyric* of 297 [supra p.58]. The Scots on Campbell's analysis would thus appear to be as indigenous as the Picts. Therefore from the point of view of the Romans, when they are referring to Picts and Caledonians, the tribes north of Hadrian's Wall, they are apparently including the Scots. They are effectively just one more tribal grouping in the north of Britain. Far too much effort has gone into trying to understand Scotland's past on the basis of differences assumed to have existed because different languages were spoken. The fact that the Picts spoke a P-Celtic form, and the Scots a Q-Celtic form of the same language group has led to all sorts of assumptions of difference, particularly in the light of the misapprehension about the founding of Dalriada. The whole modern notion of pan-Celticism which suggest there is some sort of ongoing cultural homogeneity between the peoples of Scotland, Ireland, Cornwall and Brittany because they all spoke, or speak Celtic languages is a modern fantasy. James [1999 *passim*] has shown this idea of 'the Celtic world' to be based on ideas no older than the beginning of the 18th century. However, recognising that the Scots were as indigenous as the Picts and that they were both part of the tribal culture referred to by the Romans as Pictish is a step towards gaining a more cohesive picture of Scotland in the First Millennium.

It is with the first mention of the Scots that we are introduced to what has become known as the Barbarian Conspiracy:

When the Picts, Attacotti, and Scots, after killing a general and a count, were devastating Britain without resistance, Count Theodosius routed them and took their booty.

[Ammianus 1940, p.51]

This is dated to 367/8CE and it appears that the Picts and Scots along with the as yet unidentified tribes of the Attacotti had crossed Hadrian's

Wall and raided deep into England, and Frere [1978, p.340] tells us that 'they had broken and immobilised the Army of Britain'. This event is generally known as the Barbarian Conspiracy and it is notable that while the Picts and Scots were attacking over Hadrian's Wall, and by sea, there were simultaneous attacks in Germania [Ammianus 1939, p.589]. There were also attacks by other tribes, Saxons and Franks, on Roman locations in the east of England and the coast of Gaul [*Ibid*, p.53]. Given that we know how long contact between Continental peoples and the natives of north Britain had been going on [supra, Chapter 1] the possibility that these attacks were part of some sort of sustained and organised campaign must be considered. This may have meant no more than an agreement between the various peoples to attack simultaneously and need not suggest any form of unified command structure amongst the 'barbarians'.

Just because the Picts and the Germanic tribes were pagan, non-literate and did not dwell in urban environments does not mean they were either stupid or ignorant. Sadly too many commentators have acted as if this was a given. Again the emphasis on linguistics that has coloured much of the interpretation of Scotland's past has tended to obscure such possibilities. The idea that linguistic boundaries are like those of nation states is untenable and the similarity of tribal society in north Britain and the nearby Continent – with both societies essentially being composed of pastoral, warrior, kin-based polities – combined with proof of long-term cultural contact, means these people were more than capable of regular communication with each other and the possibility of close cultural contact through trading and even going so far as inter-marriage is impossible to rule out. The corollary of this is that people speaking the same language were often enemies. This is shown in the survival of the cateran raiding tradition among the clans of Scotland into almost modern times. It is impossible to prove that in the 360s the Picts – from the Roman perspective, all the tribes of Scotland – and the Saxons – another catch-all Roman term apparently referring to north-western European peoples – were working in conjunction against the Romans, but equally there are no secure grounds for rejecting the possibility.

Smyth says:

This assault is connected in the archaeological record with repairs to Pennine forts. The evidence suggests that attack from the north was a signal for disgruntled Brigantian enclaves to turn against their local Roman garrisons. Continued political unrest was the reason why these forts were maintained in the first place until the final withdrawal of garrisons from the Pennines which began as early as the reign of Magnus Maximus in the late 380s.

[1984, p.6]

The response of the Emperor Valentian to the situation in Britain was to send Theodosius, a veteran military commander. Ammianus tells us that Theodosius

... put to flight various tribes which an insolence fostered by impunity was inflaming with a desire to attack the Romans, he completely restored the cities and strongholds which had been founded to secure a long period of peace but had suffered repeated misfortunes.

[1939, III, p.133]

The tone here is one that finds later echo in the attitude of British Army officers towards the native peoples of many different parts of the British Empire. From an indigenous point of view the insolence is on the Roman side. This period has been interpreted by some as a complete restoration of Roman control over at least southern Scotland, and Frere wrote:

Claudian hints at naval activity in the far north, and victorious terms must have been dictated, for the Notitia (Roman military record) subsequently records four regiments of Attacotti in imperial service on the Continent.

[1978, p.341]

Given that we still do not know who the Attacotti were, this is quite an assumption. If there was co-ordination between British and Continental tribes, it is not beyond possibility that the Attacotti were in fact a Germanic-speaking tribe from the other side of the North Sea. St Jerome writing in the late fourth century mentions seeing Attacotti in Roman service in Gaul. We have no direct references to indigenous tribes from the north of Britain serving with the Romans though there is of course abundant evidence for them hiring troops from amongst the Germanic-speaking tribes. Whatever the actual situation, Frere prefers to think that the Romans must have been victorious in the north. The evidence is far from conclusive. Claudian says in his *Panegyric on the Fourth Consulship of the Empire Honorius* of 398:

Twas he (Theodosius) who pitched his camp amid the snows of Caledonia, who never doffed his helmet for all the heat of a Libyan summer, who struck terror into the Moors, brought into subjection the coasts of Britain and with equal success laid waste the north and the south. What avail against him the eternal snows, the frozen air, the uncharted sea. The Orcades ran red with Saxon slaughter; Thule was warm with the blood of Picts; ice-bound Hibernia wept for the heaps of slain Scots...

[1923, p.287]

Panegyrics were not history and must be treated cautiously. Here we have Saxons in Orkney and Hibernia weeping for the Scots. Within a few lines the poet brings in references to the Gorgon and the Gardens of the Hesperides, all very well for a literary panegyric but not necessarily helpful in trying to get a clear picture of what was happening in Scotland at the end of the fourth century. What seems clear is that there was a concerted attack from the north, coinciding with similar raids on the Continent and that the raiders soon went back north to where they came from. This again is easily understood in terms of tribal behaviour. The warriors from the northern tribes were certainly always happy to give the Romans a bloody nose and consistently resisted their incursions but their primary interest in raiding south was personal, or even family, gain and not conquest or territorial expansion. This centrality of plunder to tribal raiding persisted for more than another millennium in the Highlands of Scotland and once they had gathered as much as they could carry they would naturally head home. This cannot be construed as in any way similar to a Roman campaign of conquest or the activities of an army based in a nation state. These were tribal warriors and Frere's notion of them accepting terms is dubious on several grounds. For this to happen they would have had to be defeated in battle or otherwise forced to do a deal. How did this happen? We do not know. Would there have been any of the tribal chiefs whose word would have bound other chiefs and warriors who were not his kin? This seems unlikely at this period for in all of the Roman texts we never hear of any specific leader after Calgacus.

Most of the Roman texts are either literary works or clear propaganda and must be treated with a great deal of circumspection. Contemporary sources regarding events within Roman society are much more detailed and as with Tacitus' account of his father-in-law's campaign, the focus of Roman writers was their own society which provided their audience.

Even if Theodosius had carried out a punitive expedition as far as Orkney and Shetland there is little reason to suppose this was any more effective in controlling the north than earlier attempts. Smyth points out that Britannia Inferior, today England north of the Humber, was

> ... a buffer zone designed to protect the towns and villages of southern Britain not only from the Caledonii and Maetae of the far north, but also for rebellious British tribes in the Pennines and Cheviots.
>
> [1984, p.13]

Attacks like those of Theodosius might best be seen as attempts to stem further raids from the north by discouraging the Picts. There is no evidence to show that the northern tribes were ever bribed or that they paid tribute. No Roman source mentions hostages held by the Romans from among the tribes north of Hadrian's Wall to try to ensure peace, though this was common practice throughout the Empire.

In the year 383CE the instability at the heart of the Roman Empire once more caused political disruption. Yet another Roman soldier, Magnus Maximus, decided to use Britain as a base for launching a bid to be Emperor. Like others before him he headed to the Continent to further his ambitions and the troops he took with him obviously left the British defences weakened. According to Frere [1987, p.354–5] he returned the following year to deal with the disruption that had arisen on his departure. Frere tells us that 'we may suppose' that his main purpose was to support friendly kingdoms of the Votadini and the tribes in Strathclyde. He goes further to suggest that a friendly relationship was also developed amongst the Novantae of south-west Scotland. Apart from the obvious fact that kingdoms in Scotland at this time are anachronistic, the evidence for this does not exist. Again there is the supposition on the part of a British historian that things 'must' have been that way because of the power and grandeur of the Roman Empire. Some archaeological or historical data might help. He does note that by this point the Picts and the Irish were raiding from the sea, by-passing Hadrian's Wall. This suggests that there was no longer a Roman fleet off Britain and this situation would allow of small-scale raiding without the necessity of tribal war-bands gathering together to attack and overrun the garrisons of the wall. However he does refer to 'the philo-Roman kingdoms of the Lowlands' [*Ibid*, p.355] which is frankly ridiculous. The basic tribal nature of society in many parts of Scotland continued well past this period and there is no evidence for extensive Roman influence, never mind the development of some sort of would-be Imperial behaviour amongst the tribes. The suggestion that there was, is a perfect example of what I have referred to as the Imperial mindset.

A decade later we have Stilicho, a Roman general, having to head north again. The poet Claudian writing soon after the event wrote the following in or around 400CE:

> The Saxon is conquered and the seas safe; the Picts have been defeated and Britain is secure.
>
> [1922, p.169]

For people who kept on being defeated, the Picts and their associates do not seem to have learned the lesson! However troops were needed back in Italy which was being attacked on a range of fronts, and by 407CE the Romans retreated from the whole of Britain. For over four centuries they had ruled the greater part of England, creating a rich agricultural province in the south to help feed their Empire. They had mounted many an attack to the north of Hadrian's Wall but had always been forced to retreat behind it. The Picts had kept them out and once they were gone there is no reason to assume that the native tribes did anything other than to continue their traditional way of life, which, though undoubtedly disrupted by the Romans, survived the experience. Citing archaeological evidence Edrich makes the following point:

> ... the absence of any indication of an influx of Samian ware to Traprain Law before or immediately after the periods of Roman occupation of Lowland Scotland in the first and second centuries is a strong argument against the existence of any well-established, extensive and long-term Roman native trade relations. More specifically it militates against regular trading contacts beyond the

frontier, which has long been held (e.g. Frere 1987, 286), based as Breeze (1982, 169) noted, as much on faith as direct evidence.

[2000, pp.452–3]

Whether or not there was ever any economic reasoning behind Roman expansion into Scotland the suggestion here is that the situation never was stable enough for any type of formal or friendly relationship between the tribal peoples of southern Scotland and the Romans who were set on conquering them. Edrich goes on to tell us,

> If we further accept that native peoples in Scotland were never integrated into the pre-Roman Celtic perimeter and thus were not accustomed to a market economy or coin use, then it becomes more difficult to believe the short presence of Roman military forces led to far-reaching changes in the cultural and economic organisation of indigenous native tribes.
>
> [*Ibid*, p.454]

With the withdrawal of Roman troops from Britain a new factor began to come into play. Smyth tells us [*Ibid*, p.19] that Germanic mercenaries, who had been under the control of the Romans at York, were joined by relations from the Continent. This grouping in time created Deira, an early type of kingdom which merged later with another Anglian kingdom, Bernicia to form Northumbria. The effects of the development of Northumbria were to have far-reaching consequences throughout the whole of Britain. The Anglian tribes who built the kingdom of Northumbria have in the past often been seen as part of an Anglo-Saxon invasion. Designating people culturally or ethnically by the language they speak is not particularly helpful in our understanding of the past and recent scholarship has begun to see the idea of an Anglo-Saxon invasion as untenable. John T Koch put it thus:

> Historians now generally understand that the decisive post-Roman 'invitation' of Anglo-Saxon soldiery by Vortigern... was a mere continuation of a long-standing Romano-British defence policy which had been expanded in the last century of Roman rule.
>
> [1997, p.xx]

Vortigern is the chieftain who is said by the sixth century monk Gildas to have invited the Angles, led by Hengist and Horsa, into Britain. Koch goes on to tell us

> It is fundamentally wrong, and in fact ludicrous, to conceive of the English settlements and expansion as a great war of some 300 years in duration in which a monolithic Britonnic nation purposefully resisted the advance of a comparable monolithic Germanic invader.
>
> [*Ibid*, p.xlii]

The idea of the Anglo-Saxon invasion of England no longer stands up but the predominantly Anglian tribes who settled over time in the north-east of England developed a new type of society which changed Britain forever and caused great trouble to all of the tribal peoples to the north. These Angles, initially a tribal people themselves, underwent a drastic change as the result of becoming mercenary Roman troops, changes that had a spectacular domino effect on their neighbours. Koch rightly points out that the idea of a monolithic Britonnic nation is inherently implausible but with the development of the Northumbrian state, or polity, the movement towards kingdoms or nation states took a significant step forward.

CHAPTER FOUR

Kinship not kingship

FOR THE PERIOD AFTER the departure of the Romans in the early years of the fourth century we are reliant upon a range of different sources to tell us what was going on in Britain as a whole. None of these sources are truly contemporary. We have the writings of Gildas from around 540CE, Bede's *History of the English Church and People* written around 730CE and the *Historia Brittonum* composed by the monk Nennius in the late eighth or early ninth century. The focus of all three is essentially defined by their authors' roles as officials of the Christian Church. Additionally there are the Lives of various saints, again none of which are contemporary and which of course are propagandistic rather than historical in intent. The saints' Lives were meant to strengthen and expand Christianity and where lacking corroboration must be treated very carefully. As an example, the battle of magic between Columba and the Druid Broichan at King Bruide's Pictish centre in Inverness is presented by Adomnan in his *Life of Columba* [Adomnan URL] as an illustration of Christian supremacy, with no awareness of the irony, implicit to modern readers, of a Christian saint indulging in magic to outwit a pagan enemy. Miracles occur regularly in saints' Lives and are often indistinguishable from other types of non-Christian magic. The focus of all such material is totally religious and any historical or political material that we can extract from them must be treated carefully. In Scotland the most significant saints are Ninian, Kentigern and Columba. There are also various folklore and later literary sources referring to the figure of Arthur in the fifth century. Although the widespread popularity of the figure of 'King Arthur' in medieval literature can be traced back to the, at times, fantastical works of the 12th century Welsh monk, Geoffrey of Monmouth, the widespread existence of localised material from place names and oral traditions referring to Arthur shows that he had a strong place within the culture of diverse communities throughout Britain, including most parts of Scotland. Place names and stories relating to Arthur are found in widely divergent areas where P-Celtic was spoken.

Gildas, Nennius and Bede are not overly concerned with Scotland. Like the Roman sources which were essentially propagandistic, these writers have a perspective that is not sympathetic to the Picts, or Scots, in that they are writing from an explicitly religious viewpoint. Gildas in particular must be treated very carefully indeed. His *The Ruin of Britain* (*De Excidio Britonum*) written in the first half of the sixth century, is a wild polemical rant against the contemporary state of affairs in Britain, written from the perspective of a devout, if not fanatical Christian monk. His basic concern seems to be the godlessness of society around him and if he were not the only literary source available for the period, far less reliance would be put on him due to his blatant bias and overtly Christian agenda. It is from Gildas that we get one of the most memorable descriptions of the tribes of northern Britain. Writing of the early years of the fifth century he tells us:

> As the Romans went home, there eagerly emerged from the coracles that had carried them across the sea-valleys the foul hordes of Scots and Picts, like dark throngs of worms who wriggle out of fissures in the rock when the sun is high and the weather grows warm.
>
> [1978, p.23]

Despite the florid language, and there is much more in the same vein, Gildas' tone tells us that in his time the fear of the northern tribes was very much extant and it is interesting that he links the Picts and Scots together much as earlier Roman commentators had always divided the raiders from the north in two, Caledonians and Maetae, Dicalydones and Verturiones. Generally, to date, this division has been seen as happening either side of The Mounth, the spur of the Grampians that approaches the sea near Stonehaven, though in the light of what is suggested here, such a division may well have been along the Forth–Clyde line. Watson makes the point that it was quite possible that Gildas, writing in the monastery at Llandaff, now part of modern Cardiff, had direct experience of attack by Pictish raiders. He tells us that

> The book of Llandaff gives details of the cruelty of the Picts in the course of their raids in the coast of Wales, and of their insults to the clergy.
>
> [1925, p.14]

This is supported in the *Life of St Gildas* by Caradoc, written *c*.1130–50, in which he says

> ... pirates came from the islands of Orcades, who harassed him snatching off his servants from him when at their duties, and carrying them off to exile, along with spoils and all the furniture of their dwelling.
>
> [Caradoc 10, URL]

Watson links these attacks to other sea-going incursions by the Picts a century later. This shows that the raiding propensities of the northern peoples continued long after the departure of Roman troops. While Caradoc's Life is written half a millennium after the fact, there is a strong likelihood that the author had access to earlier texts and there is no perceptible advantage to be gained either by him, or the author of the *Book of Llandaff*, which survives in a 12th century manuscript, inventing such raids. We can therefore accept this as further proof of the ongoing raids from the north, and that in all likelihood in Gildas' time these raiders were non-Christian. Gildas also makes an interesting point about the Picts and Scots:

> They were in some extent different in their customs, but they were in perfect accord in their greed for bloodshed; and they were readier to cover their villainous faces with hair than their private parts and neighbouring regions with clothes.
>
> [*Ibid*]

Perhaps he is referring to the difference in language but he is undoubtedly linking them together, both as raiders and as people whose personal habits were outrageous to him as a chaste and devout monk. From a southern perspective the Picts were no doubt primarily seen as savage raiders coming from the north to loot and pillage. This echoes earlier references like Ammianus Marcellinus in linking the Picts and Scots as, at the very least, working together on raids to the south.

He also writes of the incoming of the Saxons whom he sees, like the northern raiders, as instruments of God's will to punish the increasingly godless inhabitants of England. He states that they came initially in three keels, or warships [*Ibid*, p.26], and goes on to describe them as having destroyed all the major towns in the country and spread devastation everywhere [*Ibid*, p.27]. He then tells us of a major battle at Badon Hill where the indigenous people rallied against the invaders under the leadership of one Ambrosius Aurelianus and turned the tide, eventually securing victory as the 'siege of Badon Hill' [*Ibid*, p.28]. As noted above, modern scholarship rejects the idea of an organised invasion from the east but there is little doubt that in the period following the retreat of the Romans, raiders attacked England much more than they had while the Romans were still there and that these raiders came both from the north and the east. Ambrosius Aurelianus, whom he mentions as the leader of the native people, is said to have been a Roman [*Ibid*] and many commentators have seen him as being the same person as Arthur and thus in some way a Roman-style commander. While this seems to be a popular current theory there is no evidence to support this and, as I have pointed out elsewhere [McHardy 2001] both the provenance and distribution of stories concerning Arthur can be interpreted differently.

Before looking at what Nennius has to say, and the evidence from the various saints' Lives about this period, we should look again at the basic social structure of the Pictish, and Scottish tribes. It seems clear that their social organisation was to a considerable extent structured round the reality that all of the physically capable men of the tribe were warriors and that they expressed this through the practice of raiding. Raiding was more than just the accumulation of goods. It served both as a way of training young warriors and allowed the expression of the full range of the mature warrior's skills and talents. This meant that they had to have some sort of structure for such raiding. This, as has been noted above, did not necessarily mean that the chief of a tribe always led raids or was the commander in battle. The differentiation between raiding and a battle is in itself significant. The practice of raiding meant that there would always be the possibility of fighting but above and beyond that, since at least the arrival of the Romans, there was always the possibility of the need to enter into battle to defend the tribe, possibly in conjunction with warriors from other tribes. Just as Calgacus leading the massed ranks against the Romans at Mons Graupius was not designated as any kind of aristocrat so we must look at the leaders of raids, or even campaigns, as warriors who were chosen on merit rather than inheriting their status. As Hedeager tells us, within tribal societies

Authority is linked to the office, not the person, and he is therefore not irreplaceable but can be removed from office in certain
circumstances.

[1992, p.30]

This is an aspect of tribal existence that continued amongst the
Highland clans into modern times. It seems eminently clear that in the
fifth century in Scotland there were no such things as kings as the term is
nowadays understood. A term used by Broun [2007], 'head of the kindred'
is an apt way of describing the role of the leaders amongst the different
tribes. Part of our problem in dealing with the past is that the people at
the head of various polities in the early period, when referred to by monks,
are generally called in Latin, *rex*. This has been generally accepted as
meaning king and the Celtic terms *ri* in P-Celtic and *righ* in Q-Celtic are
assumed to have the same meaning. This makes little sense regarding
tribal societies. The Romans had clear ideas about what kings were and
we should remember that the monks who gave us our early literary
sources of history within the British Isles in the First Millennium were
literate in Latin. That literacy was developed from the study of Roman
texts and combined with the regular appearance of kings in the Christian
bible led to assumptions about the native people that have coloured
interpretations ever since. As Hedeager points out, the leader of a tribe
takes his authority from the office of chief, not just because of his birth,
though it is true to say that the chiefs in most tribal societies are drawn
from a restricted group, who are essentially defined as being the closest
blood relations to the predecessor from whom the entire tribe claim
descent. Hedeager also tells us

... in tribal society, that is in a chiefdom, both production and
reproduction are organised through kinship... Control is rooted
in the kinship structure, which has not yet been transformed into
a class structure that permits an upper class to withdraw from
the traditional kinship duties.

[*Ibid*, p.88]

The key to understanding the Picts, certainly in the early period – always
remembering that kinship structures survived as the basis of society in
Galloway and the Borders till the late medieval period and even later in

the Highland clan system – is therefore kinship not kingship. In fact until considerably later than the fifth century I suggest we should be looking at Scottish society as a series of chiefdoms not kingdoms. This influences how we should interpret the Pictish King Lists, for the idea of chief amongst chiefs which is one reading of the term *Ard-ri*, as opposed to high king, found in Gaelic sources, is totally different from the generally accepted idea of a king, with its connotations of primogeniture, feudalism and the pernicious idea that some human beings are born better than others, not through genetically inherited talents, but simply because of their blood-line. The irrelevance of such an idea within a society where the uniting mechanism is a belief in the shared descent from a common ancestor is obvious.

Within the tribal structure the reasons for fighting are also distinct. Hedeager tells us:

> All wars and battles have a motive. The tribal warrior will fight first and foremost for his own prestige and his clan's, be that through some particularly heroic action or through the winning of valuables which also create prestige when given away. The motive for battle thus hardly passes beyond the reproduction and prestige of the clan or tribe, and so its military effectiveness is likewise limited.
>
> [*Ibid*, p.91]

The concept of raiding for booty which can then be given away for prestige amongst one's kin is totally different from the idea of raiding to advance one's own wealth, power or territory. In fact wealth within the tribe, except for such well documented practices as the ostentation of chiefs in Highland society where the chief was the symbol of and for the rest of the clan, does not appear to have been particularly important for the individual. In the times before the introduction of a money economy this would be particularly true. The point about the lack of perceived military effectiveness is also pertinent. Time and again, tribal groups, as in the later Highlands, raided each other without ever trying to conquer their target, who in different circumstances might well be a friend. The function of battle within tribal societies is different from that of nation states or kingdoms. Hedeager makes this explicit:

The true subordination of a conquered territory with a view to making the population tributary is irreconcilable with a political structure which is based on kinship alone. Territorial conquest and the subordination of larger groups of people can first be effected when the conquerors have at their disposal a political and military power apparatus which can be introduced to follow up the victory. However plundering, pillage, slave-raiding and the extortion of 'payments for peace' do not require the same power apparatus. The profit motive here is 'cash' and the relevant military organization need not comprise anything more than a series of individuals with a leader, possibly organised in some form of war band. Their tactic is surprise attack. Their mobility is great, and time, place and circumstances are all the attackers are concerned with.

[*Ibid*, p.92]

He goes on to contrast this with pitched battles fought till one side is totally victorious, when the motive is territorial expansion, religious conversion or command of resources such as trading routes, metal deposits etc, making the point that when this happens battle becomes dreadfully bloodthirsty and effectively suggests that it develops into what we nowadays think of as war. He compares this, generally later development of tribal warfare, with the behaviour of the raiding party, telling us the following:

With this, the character of battle changes; it is now far from the athletic, often ritualised armed sports displays of the tribal societies in which death is the exception. Now a man strikes the enemy instead of taking part in a dance. In addition to the two above mentioned motives for battle, the economic and the prestige-related, there is the religious motive. Through rituals, dreams, prophecies and so on, the gods can declare that a particular battle is to be undertaken or avoided, that a particular person shall be leader etc.

[*Ibid*]

The idea of fighting to the death was not necessarily the norm as he suggests, though the possibility always existed and even as late as the dawn of the 18th century in Scotland there is evidence of a raid that culminated in a single combat between representatives of the raiders and their victims, to decide who took the spoils, but which then turned into all-out battle in which the raiders were all killed [McHardy 2004, p.48ff]. There were undoubtedly models of ideal, or accepted behaviour, but they were not always adhered to.

The point about the use of dreams and prophecies is also particularly apposite to the situation in Scotland, as we shall see when we discuss the role of Columba in the late sixth century. That religion can be a cause of battle is a truism in the modern world, but it is also perhaps particularly relevant in the centuries after the Romans withdrew. We have seen that the picture we have of the period has been created mainly from works written by priests or monks but the idea that they are in some way commentators outside the politics of their time, or the times on which they are commenting, is not sustainable. It is from the early fifth century however that the role of the Christian Church begins to directly affect the existence of the Pictish tribes.

King Arthur

Elsewhere [McHardy 2001] I have looked in depth at the possible Scottish provenance of the putatively historical Arthur. The figure of Arthur, surviving in a variety of Welsh language sources predating the 12th century works of Geoffrey of Monmouth which gave rise to the European popularity of the Arthurian story, appears to be common to all the P-Celtic speaking peoples of Britain and Brittany. This of course includes the tribal peoples of southern Scotland, the Damnonii, Novantae, Selgovae and Votadini of Ptolemy. It also includes the tribal peoples to the north of the Forth–Clyde line, who later coalesce into the Pictish nation. The Roman designation of all the tribes as Pictish underlines the cultural cohesion that a shared language, economic structure and social structure suggest. This includes the Scots in Argyll, who differed in having a common language with the inhabitants of Ireland, with whom they shared at least some mythological and legendary material, while still being socially, economically and politically little different from their neighbours, the Picts.

In the oral tradition stories are told within the language of the audience, something particularly important for children in pre-literate societies where all knowledge has to be passed on either by the spoken word or by example. In order to give children a sense of identity as members of tribal society, myths and legends were told as happening within the environment they inhabited. This is why there are so many variants of Arthurian stories all over Britain. None of these locations has any better claim to being the origin centre than any other. All the P-Celtic speaking peoples had the story of Arthur, though by the time many of the tales were being consigned to paper in the 12th century in Welsh, received opinion suggests the P-Celtic language dialects of Scotland were either extinct or close to it. The earliest known reference to Arthur, in the poem *The Gododdin*, written around 600CE, probably in Edinburgh, survives as part of Welsh literature, despite its Scottish origin. There are also many references in early Welsh poetry and other literary sources derived from the oral tradition of the *Gwr Y Gogledd*, the Men of the North. These are the tribal peoples of southern and central Scotland who in the centuries after the collapse of the Roman Empire grew into the peoples we know of as the Gododdin, previously known to the Romans as the Votadini, and the Britons of Strathclyde. As we shall see, it is as these political entities move towards structures resembling nation states or kingdoms that the term Pict begins to be used to refer specifically to their cousins to the north. In the *Historia Brittonum,* a ninth century text generally associated with Nennius, a monk in Bangor, there is a mention of one of these northern warriors:

> Cunedda, with his twelve sons, had come before from the left-hand part, i.e. from the country which is called Manau Guotodin, 146 years before Mailcun reigned, and expelled the Scots with much slaughter from those countries, and they never returned again to inhabit them.
>
> [Nennius, URL]

This would have taken place in the early years of the fifth century and it has always been assumed that Nennius was referring to Cunedda fighting incomers from Ireland. However, I would propose that it is just as likely that he is referring to Scots from Dalriada. After all we know the nature of the geography of Argyll meant that the Scots were able sailors and the sea journey from Argyll to north Wales, while longer than from Ireland itself, is not any more difficult. It is tempting to see the invitation of warriors from the north as being due to the local people in north Wales having lost some of their fighting skills during the Roman occupation. If at this period we accept the Roman designation of Pict as referring to all the tribal peoples north of Hadrian's Wall this does not cause a problem. The tribes continued to raid each other and there are many reported instances of battles between Scot and Pict, Briton and Pict, and Briton and Scot. The fact that these terms nowadays have specific quasi-nationalistic meanings does not alter the fact that back in the fifth century the tribal warrior's loyalty was to his kin and that even the idea of nationhood, or the state, was still some way off. We must also remember that references in Irish Annals to battles in Scotland, until now always interpreted as essentially dynastic, may well have been no more than traditional raids. Without locating such sites and investigating them it is impossible to be precise as to the specific social or political function of such battles. However in societies 'addicted to raiding' it seems preferable to give the idea of raids greater weight than anachronistic ideas of dynastic struggle, certainly before the seventh century.

The area of Cunedda's origin, Manau Guotodin, is believed to be the area around the upper waters of the Firth of Forth, close to the Stirling Gap. This was part of the area occupied by the Gododdin, though the reason for its separate designation, and its extent, are as yet somewhat unclear. Cunedda's sons became founders of a dynasty, or more properly are described in later texts as having done so. The survival of such genealogies generally owes much more to the need to preserve or acquire status in contemporary society than to a wish to preserve 'history'.

CHAPTER FIVE

The coming of the monks

EARLY IN THE FIFTH century we have the arrival of a new force in Scotland which was to have a profound effect on the development of Pictish society. This was the first arrival of the Christian Church, in the person of St Ninian. It is as yet unclear whether Ninian established his foundation at Candida Casa on the north shore of the Solway Firth before or after the Romans retreated from Britain. MacQueen [1990, p.21] suggests a date between 400 and 420CE, and while today even the existence of Ninian is itself under question [Clancy 2001] there is ample archaeological evidence for Christian activity at Whithorn from the later fifth century. We are reliant on Bede, writing some 400 years later, for most of our information about Ninian and he explicitly states that he set out to convert the southern Picts. Following the suggestions above it is suggested that this should be taken as referring to the tribal, pre-Christian peoples living in Scotland south of the Forth–Clyde line, thus addressing the anomalous idea that Ninian was proselytising amongst the tribes north of the Mounth from a base on the Solway Firth miles away. This has been the standard interpretation because of what Bede wrote, viz,

> ... the provinces of the northern Picts, which are separated from those of the southern Picts by a range of steep and desolate mountains.
>
> The southern Picts are said to have abandoned the errors of idolatry long before this date, and had accepted the true Faith through the teaching of Bishop Ninian, a most revered and holy man of the British race, who had been regularly instructed in the mysteries of the Christian faith in Rome.
>
> [1955, p.143]

There is no evidence that Bede was ever in Scotland and it is quite possible that his source was describing either the mountains of the Merrick chain north of Whithorn, or even the hill-ridges of the Campsies and the Ochils, that run across central Scotland with a gap at Stirling. Both these locations would have been heavily wooded and might well appear virtually impassable to visitors. Locating the southern Picts south of the Forth–Clyde line would also account for the Pictish sculptures at Anwoth on the opposite side of Wigtown Bay from Whithorn. By the time Bede is writing, Whithorn is said to be within Bernicia, one of the early kingdoms of the Northumbrians. As we shall see the expansion of the Northumbrians through the sixth and subsequent centuries greatly altered the political make-up of southern and central Scotland and we should consider whether Bede's use of the term Picts was being applied to those tribes north of the Forth–Clyde line while in Ninian's time – immediately after the Roman withdrawal – the term was still being used of all of the people north of Hadrian's Wall. We have already considered the possibility that the general dating of Pictish symbol stones is potentially undermined by the Collessie Stone with its carving of a single warrior, so the Pictish carvings at Anwoth may well also be quite early. The Anwoth carvings are a good fit for Romilly Allen's Class 1 as they have no obvious Christian symbolism. If they are indeed pre-Christian this may well suggest a conspicuously early date if we accept the idea that Ninian had converted the people in the area by the late fifth century. Bede tells us that Ninian's church was known as *Candida Casa*, The White House because, unusually among the Britons, it was built of stone. Here he must be referring to the Britons south of Hadrian's Wall as we have no evidence of any Christian sites in Scotland prior to Whithorn. In the 12th century *Life of Ninian* by Ailred of Rievaux it is stated that the saint came from the area of the Solway Firth but we must treat this statement with caution. Ailred was writing in the 12th century at a time when control of Whithorn Abbey was an important strategic objective in the struggle to unite Scotland politically and religiously. He was a member of the Cistercian order and a supporter of the central authority of both the Roman Church and the royal house of Malcolm against the Lords of Galloway. They were trying to retain their independence and invoked the ancient religious traditions of the south west in support of their right to autonomy [Ninian URL]. It was therefore advantageous not just to claim a specific local Christian saint but possibly even exaggerate his influence to bolster that right.

Christianity had been adopted as one of the official religions of the Roman Empire as early as 314CE with the Edict of Milan issued by the Emperor Constantine and it spread rapidly throughout Roman-controlled areas. However when the Empire fell, Christianity continued to expand, often basing its localised structures on established Imperial ones e.g. the Bishoprics of York, London etc. It is therefore possible that Ninian had come under the influence of Christianity in the area where he raised his church. The existence of carved crosses and other artefacts from the fifth century at Whithorn shows that there was certainly a Christian centre there. Sadly Bede tells us little about what subsequently happened to Ninian and concentrates on the later arrival of St Columba from Ireland.

The coming of Christianity into the lands of the Pictish tribes was not necessarily peaceful. Even as late as 617CE, according to the *Annals of Ulster*, Donnan was martyred on the island of Eigg with 51 companions and it is generally accepted that the assailants were Picts. In a letter from St Patrick written around the middle of the fifth century he has the following:

> With my own hand I have written and composed these words, to be given, delivered, and sent to the soldiers of Coroticus; I do not say, to my fellow citizens, or to fellow citizens of the holy Romans, but to fellow citizens of the demons, because of their evil works. Like our enemies, they live in death, allies of the Scots and the apostate Picts. Dripping with blood, they welter in the blood of innocent Christians, whom I have begotten into the number for God and confirmed in Christ!
>
> The day after the newly baptised, anointed with chrism, in white garments (had been slain) – the fragrance was still on their foreheads when they were butchered and slaughtered with the sword by the above-mentioned people – I sent a letter with a holy presbyter whom I had taught from his childhood, clerics accompanying him, asking them to let us have some of the booty, and of the baptised they had made captives. They only jeered at them.
>
> [St Patrick, URL]

The Coroticus mentioned has been identified, tentatively, as a 'king' in either Wales or Strathclyde. Anderson notes [1990, p.143] that one early source attributes the slaughter of Donnan and his companions to the fact that they had offended a Pictish queen by taking up residence on lands where she was wont to graze her sheep. We shall return to the concept of Pictish queens later but we must treat the notion of a queen at this period with as much care as the term king. What is clear however is that the coming of Christianity into the northern part of Britain was not necessarily peaceful. It is also interesting in that the reference to the Picts as apostate suggests that whatever success Ninian had had amongst the tribes was fleeting. The reference to them as demons is reminiscent of Nennius' 'foul hordes'. There is a tradition that Patrick was born somewhere near Dumbarton, a capital of the Britons of Strathclyde, but he is associated primarily with Ireland. We therefore have evidence that suggests that the struggle between the expansionist Christian religion and native peoples adhering to their older, original beliefs carried on from the middle of the fifth to the seventh century at least. The religious beliefs of the indigenous peoples are generally referred to as pagan, a rather amorphous term, but is difficult to avoid the surmise that some of them at least would have been just as prepared to fight against the new religion attempting to supplant their beliefs, as they had been to resist Roman attempts to subjugate them. To this day there are festivities that take place annually in Scotland that have survived from pre-Christian beginnings, such as the various fire festivals, the use of sacred wells, and others [McNeill 1957, 1959 *passim*]. The idea that Christianity came into Scotland in a peaceful and inevitable fashion is of course no more than Christian propaganda and given that our universities were initially set up to educate young men for the Christian ministry it is hardly to be wondered at that this idea has permeated most treatments of our past.

Elsewhere [McHardy 2001] I have suggested that the 12 battles that Nennius said Arthur fought can be interpreted as a single campaign through southern central Scotland with the express aim of subjugating important centres of pre-Christian sacral activity. While this would locate a historical figure using the name Arthur – or having been given it – in Scotland in the sixth century, it does not affect the authenticity of oral traditions regarding Arthur in different parts of the island. The locations of these battles on this interpretation are all significantly close to sites which were used in tribal times and several of them, the Eildon Hills in the Borders, Loudon Hill in Ayrshire, Dumbarton Rock and others, have the remnants of Roman camps nearby. This suggests that such sites were perceived by the Romans as being of importance within local tribal society. As has already been noted, such sites while they may well have had some military function at varying times, would also have had significance for the large-scale gatherings, social, sacred, legal or economic that would form part of normal, if not everyday, tribal behaviour. Tribal peoples throughout the world have generally had the need for both a sacred centre for their territory and for a location, often the summit of a prominent hill, where gatherings could take place to dispense justice, anoint leaders, spiritual and temporal, perhaps allocate land use and provide a location for feasts on socially significant occasions like notable weddings or funerals, as well as hosting the great feast days of the year. This interpretation could also explain why the figure of Arthur, much of the material regarding whom clearly derives from deep in the tribal past, survived to become one of the greatest inspirational figures of all time. As a Christian victor, but one deriving from the tribal past, he would have provided a good exemplar of a winning hero for the Christians to use amongst the tribes in their ongoing campaigns of conversion.

Dates for Arthur's supposed final battle vary from around 515 through to 537 and without locating and examining the possible sites of these battles the date must remain moot. However if he had been victorious in establishing or securing Christianity within central and southern Scotland it is possible that his actions made the work of later Christian missionaries considerably easier.

Christianity brought with it attitudes and practices that were to drastically affect Pictish society. The organisational structure of the new religion shifted the focus of power within society. The religious ideas that preceded Christianity can be interpreted as being centred round a Mother Goddess type figure [McHardy 2006, 2003 *passim*]. This I have suggested was manifested in sacred activities that were essentially linked both to the small scattered communities of the Pictish tribes and to the landscape itself, where the plethora of *Pap* and *Cioch*, both meaning breast or nipple, names drawing attention to geophysical shapes that were redolent of the Goddess herself, were the focus of activities we can still discern through place names, ancient monuments, sacred wells and mythological and legendary material [McHardy 2005, chapter 12]. An example of this is the survival of an ancient idea into a 15th century Scots poem, the *Gyre-Carling*. This gigantic female, a precise match for the *Cailleach* in Q-Celtic oral tradition, was a landscape maker in many tales and in the poem and she is expressly said to have 'lut fart' North Berwick Law, one of the Paps of Lothian. Elsewhere [McHardy 2003, 2005, 2006] I have suggested that the *Carlin* and the *Cailleach* are specific, powerful, female, remnants of a one-time belief in a Mother

Goddess. The existence here of a powerful coven of witches at the turn of the 17th century may not be coincidental.

While it appears likely that the smaller communities would come together at certain special times, and at specific locations, for major festive activities, the norm I suggest would have been more localized, and thus more immediately relevant to day-to-day living. Such locations would undoubtedly have gained some of their continuing importance precisely because of their association with past activities and links to the ancestors of the contemporary tribespeople. The new religion brought in new concepts. The idea of an all powerful, often vengeful, male God was accompanied by the concept of all humans and particularly women, as being essentially sinful. This, in a society where the likelihood was that women were at the very least equal to men, but where there was belief in a Mother Goddess, and possibly some sort of matriliny, suggests major change. There were other radical changes. The old goddess was within the landscape, the new God was in some unidentified stellar heaven. This would have to mean changes in people's perceptions of both themselves and the environment they inhabited, but there were other new ideas that were to have dramatic effects.

While it is possible that Christianity was introduced alongside aspects of previous religious practice – the policy of taking over pagan precincts advocated by Pope Gregory [Bede 1955, p.86] would encourage this and similar processes can be seen in many parts of the world where Christianity has merged with previous beliefs to create specific local forms – certain of the new practices were truly revolutionary. The introduction of literacy encouraged a process of centralisation that in time led tribal politics towards the development of embryonic nation states. Literacy meant that the keeping of records of all kinds was made much easier and the hierarchic structure of the Church itself provided a model for change. The political role of the new religion was explicit and after the Synod of Whitby in 664 the loyalty to Rome, and the consequent amassing of land by the Church, this would have provided a model of behaviour that must have been attractive to those forces looking for increased centralisation as a means of combating external pressure. This I suggest was a meaningful step along the way from kinship to kingship. Sawyer, writing of the Norwegian kings Olaf Trygvasson and Olaf Harladson, says:

They had discovered what great advantages Christianity could confer on kings, and only that can explain the extraordinary ferocity with which they evangelised.

[1982, p.139]

Although the Olafs were not active till the end of the First Millennium the advantages of Christianity for centralising power would have been just as great earlier.

The introduction of literacy alone was such a major change that, even if it remained the prerogative of a very small section of society for many centuries, it could only serve to weaken traditional societal structures that had developed in a purely oral environment. Now instead of a corpus of shared stories, legends and myths that had developed within the community over a potentially very long period of time, there was a specific document that provided the moral and practical model for behaviour that was, in effect, new law. The Bible and the capacity for record keeping that arose from the Annals [see below] removed the focus of belief and morality from a shared and traditional basis that was rooted in the collective memory of the community to a fixed and external point, the Christian Bible. And the main concern of the monks, priests and bishops was not the community itself but the power and influence of their religion within it. Their education arose from texts written in highly centralised states and increasingly, particularly after Whitby, the focus of how they functioned was dictated from Rome, rather than the community in which they operated. Where the Roman Empire failed to conquer the Picts, the Christian Church succeeded.

CHAPTER SIX

Religious and political change

THE ONLY REAL CONTEMPORARY evidence we have for what was happening in Scotland in the period of the fifth to the eighth centuries comes
from Annals. These documents were created in Christian monasteries
and arose from the written tables created to calculate the correct date
for such moveable feasts as Easter. In time, the list of years and dates
began to include information considered significant by the monks creating
them. The annotations to the Annals, originally in the margins, referred
to particularly notable events within the Church or major events like
plagues or famines and to the death of persons deemed notable by the
scribes, or by those directing their efforts. The arrival of St Patrick in
Ireland in 432CE is probably entered in a later copy of the original
Annals of Ulster, but the reference to the first Saxon raid on Ireland two
years later is likely to have been written at the time. So our earliest history comes to us through a Christian filter with all the reservations that
entails. Due to a series of unfortunate later historical events, incursions
from the south by Edward I and later by Cromwell, and the vandalistic
activities of mobs in the period of the Christian Reformation in the late
16th century, no early Scottish Annals survive. We are thus forced to
rely on external sources from Ireland and to a lesser degree, England.
These sources combined with the retrospective accounts of Nennius,
Bede and Gildas do provide enough material to suggest how Pictish society
developed in the centuries after the Roman withdrawal from England.
Though the departure of the Romans removed one source of ongoing attack
on the Pictish tribes from the south, it was soon replaced by another.

The major change to the political situation in the north of Britain in
the sixth century was the rise of Northumbria, in north-eastern England.
In this area troops – who had originally been hired by the Romans from
amongst the Germanic tribes to defend Hadrian's Wall against the Picts
– had settled. This would appear to be a case of using tribal warriors against
tribal warriors. Tacitus mentioned similarities between the Caledonians
and the people in Germania when he wrote, 'The reddish hair and large
limbs of the Caledonians proclaim a German origin...' [Agricola 11, p.61]

and their employment by the Romans is a clear case of fighting fire with fire. Marsden, talking of the first known dynasty among the Northumbrian Angles, that of Ida in the mid sixth century, tells us:

> The eventual dominance of Ida's dynasty (he was the first of the Northumbrian kings) can already be detected in its earliest years, but can only be explained against an outline of the nature of kings and kingship in the English settlements and in the continental Germanic homelands. The word 'king' derives from Old English *cyning* and the idea of 'kingship' seems to have been first imported into these islands with the tribal war bands settled here by Rome as foederati and laeti.
>
> The primitive continental form of kingship was, according to Bede's evidence from seventh century Northumbrian missionaries in Old Saxony, a temporary military command brought into effect only in time of war, when tribal war bands chose a warlord from their chieftains as military overlord for the duration of the campaign. When such Germanic war bands were settled in Britain they were obliged to fight whenever required by the Romans... and were consequently moved on to a full-time war footing. The role of their warrior-king was similarly transferred from a temporary to a full time basis.
>
> [1992, p.30]

This I suggest is an extremely significant point. It is probable that the tribal warrior systems of the incomers were originally little different from the Pictish tribes they were hired to combat. It was this full time professional role as soldiers that makes a fundamental change to contemporary society. In the period after the Roman withdrawal in the early years of the fifth century, the Germanic mercenaries who stayed behind, some probably already settled in the area after serving their time in Roman service, as was the norm, were already living in a different form of society than the tribes to the north. There the role of the war-band leader continued for some time but the rise of Ida and his sons created something that was moving towards our modern idea of a nation state. The Angles of Northumbria effectively moved from a kinship-based society to one based on kingship, even if Ida himself was little more than, in Marsden's words, 'an aggrandised war-lord' [*Ibid*]. The reality that tribal raiding continued for more than a millennium in the lands further to the north shows the tenacity of the tribal kinship system but those peoples who were neighbours to the expansionist Northumbrian Angles were, over the ensuing centuries, forced to respond to the new threat. That the Northumbrians were set on expanding their own territory is clear from subsequent events even if in the long term they were no more successful than the Romans in their attempts at conquering the Picts. Their repeated attempts to annexe the lands to the north would appear to have continued the process of uniting the northern tribes that had started with the battle of Mons Graupius.

Initially the Northumbrians formed into two separate polities, with Ida controlling Bernicia, based around the great fortress of Bamburgh a few miles south of Lindisfarne, and possibly originally part of Gododdin lands. To the south, based around York, was Deira, suggested by some to have been created by another *cyning,* Soemil, possibly as early as the fifth century. The two entities were to unite in 603 under Aethelfrith of Northumbria who married Acha, daughter of Aelle of Deira. However by this time there had been other developments to the north, which were likewise to bring great changes.

In the second half of the sixth century we begin to hear about Pictish 'kings' who may have been historical. There is a reference in the *Annals of Ulster* for the year 546:

> the flight before Máelchá's son; and the death of Gabrán son of Domangart.
>
> [*Annals of Ulster,* URL 546.1]

Adomnan, one of Columba's successors as the Abbot of Iona, writing in the later years of the seventh century tells us Bridei Mac Maelchon was king of the Picts. Gabran was a Dalriadan but it is notable that the reference in the *Annals of Ulster* refers to neither Gabran or Bridei as a king. Adomnan tells us that the saint on one of his visits to King Bruide at Inverness that he was 'in the presence of the ruler of the Orcades' [*Ibid*]. This has been interpreted as meaning that the ruler of the Orcades was not only a king but was in some sense a sub-king to Bridei. However this is not stated explicitly, though Bridei is referred to as a king. By Adomnan's time, under the pressure for Northumbrian expansion it seems likely that a centralised kingship was beginning to form amongst the Picts. It is this process, the development of kingship in response to external aggression that I suggest led to the formation of the Pictish kingdom north of the Forth–Clyde line and in Columba's role in the Dalriada kingship process we can perhaps discern how the Church would have played a part in such a development. By the end of the seventh century the Church in Scotland was under the control of Rome and was much more centralised and rigidly structured than the original Columban Church had been. This must have affected how the leaders of the Picts reacted to their own political situation.

The Scots were perhaps already a more coherently structured grouping prior to this. The document known as the *Senchus FerN'Alban*, generally believed to be based on a 10th century original but with material from earlier describes the Dalriadan Scots as being divided into three main groupings, the *Cenel nGabrain*, the *Cenel nOengusa* and *Cenel Loairnd*. These terms clearly conform to the fundamental tribal idea of claiming descent from a common ancestor, these here being Gabrain, Oengusa and Loairnd, with Gabrain possibly being the father of that Aedan crowned as king by Columba in the sixth century. It is hardly a stretch to see the linkage between the concepts of *Cenel* and the *clan* in later times. This is clear evidence that the basic tribal system of the Q-Celtic speaking tribes of Dalriada survived into at least the sixth if not the seventh century, though like the Pictish tribal system it was in a process of change. Adomnan specifically tells us that

> On another occasion, when this eminent man was staying in the Hinba island (Eilean-na-Naoimh), he saw, on a certain night, in a mental ecstasy, an angel sent to him from heaven, and holding in his hand a book of glass, regarding the appointment of kings. Having received the book from the hand of the angel, the venerable man, at his command, began to read it; and when he was reluctant to appoint Aidan king, as the book directed, because he had a greater affection for Iogenan his brother, the angel, suddenly stretching forth his hand, struck the saint with a scourge, the livid marks of which remained in his side all the days of his life. And he added these words: 'Know for certain,' said he, 'that I am sent to thee by God with the book of glass, that in accordance with the words thou hast read therein, thou mayest inaugurate Aidan into the kingdom; but if thou refuse to obey this command,

I will strike thee again.' When therefore this angel of the Lord had appeared for three successive nights, having the same book of glass in his hand, and had repeated the same commands of the Lord regarding the appointment of the same king, the saint, in obedience to the command of the Lord, sailed across to the Iouan island (Hy, now Iona), and there ordained, as he had been commanded, Aidan to be king, who had arrived at the same time as the saint. During the words of consecration, the saint declared the future regarding the children, grandchildren and great-grand-children of Aidan, and laying his hand upon his head, he consecrated and blessed him.

[Adomnan, URL]

Following the accepted mode of writing the life of a saint, Adomnan wishes to make it clear that Columba was merely following the word of the Lord by installing Aedan as King of Dalriada. There is clearly some question as to precisely what is meant here by king but at the very least it would appear to refer to a position at the head of Dalriadan society, even if it were that of an over-chief or high-chief with all the connotations that would have within a non-aristocratic tribal society. It certainly seems to be more than the head of a specific kindred. However we are entitled to question Columba's motives on the basis of what we know of his life before he came to Scotland. He was in fact sent into exile from Ireland after taking part in the Battle of Cul Drebene, registered in the *Annals of Ulster* in 561. This battle, which appears to have been fought between the northern and southern branches of the Ui Neill clan, resulted in victory for Columba's northern sept and the *Annals of Ulster* say that 3,000 men died in the battle, claiming also that the northerners won through the prayers of Colum Cille, St Columba. Adomnan's projection of Columba as a man of peace and a model of sanctity does not stand up and Smyth says of him,

Columba... was not only a member of the warrior aristocracy but he continued into the holy part of his life to maintain an abiding interest in the affairs of... warlords, advising them how to behave, predicting how they would die and even showing a warrior's own fascination with the outcome of their battles. Equally significant for this warrior aspect of Columba's life is the early evidence for his cult procuring victory in war. With the suppression of the pagan war-gods such as the Celtic Badb and the Germanic Woden, the warrior-caste desperately needed a substitute for their old victory gods. Saints of Columba's hot blood fitted the bill for this role much more than the figure of Christ who preached mercy and dissociation from violence.

[Smyth 1984, pp.96–7]

While I would dispute the very notion of a warrior aristocracy and the idea of a separate warrior caste within society in tribal Scotland in this period, the thrust of this is unarguable. Columba was what we today might think of as a politician. Clearly within contemporary society he would have to be prepared to regularly deal with men for whom violence was not only an accepted, but a welcome aspect of existence, but the evidence suggests he was, at heart, one of them. However his role in the selection of Aedan suggests something further. Here we are seeing a clear attempt at political manipulation and in the light of contemporary events this is extremely significant. We hear nothing of him being able to influence matters amongst the Picts to the same extent but Adomnan does tell us of how he defeated a powerful druid at Bruide's court. It is also of interest that Adomnan's own political agenda seems to have been successful – Columba is not only Scotland's patron saint but he is so despite the presence of other early Christian missionaries to the lands of both the Scots and the Picts such as Comgall, Brendan and Moluag, all of whom came from Ireland in the same period. Lynch [1992, p.34] makes the point that there was a specific rivalry with that other early missionary, Donnan, who according to the *Annals of Ulster* was martyred on Eigg in 617CE along with 150 companions, presumably at the hands of Picts who were still adherents of the pre-Christian religion.

Before this however there were a couple of significant battles to the south that must be considered. The poem *The Gododdin* has already been mentioned and is generally thought to refer to a battle between warriors of the Gododdin and Northumbrians to the south. The acceptance of the location of this battle at Catterick in England has not however been substantiated and the name *Catraeth* itself translates as the Battle of Raeth. Generally located in the closing years of the sixth century this interpretation has some support from another reported battle slightly earlier. This is the Siege of Lindisfarne mentioned in the *Historia Brittonum*:

Hussa reigned seven years. Against him fought four kings, Urien, and Ryderch Hen, and Guallauc, and Morcant. Theodoric fought bravely, together with his sons, against that Urien. But at that time sometimes the enemy and sometimes our countrymen were defeated, and he shut them up three days and three nights in the island of Metcaut; and whilst he was on an expedition he was murdered, at the instance of Morcant, out of envy, because he possessed so much superiority over all the kings in military science.

[*Historia*, URL]

Metcaut is the island of Lindisfarne, best known as a religious site but here being used as a fort. This battle is generally placed in 590CE and it is of particular interest that the 'kings' mentioned are from what I have suggested are tribal groupings to the north and the west. Urien came from Rheged, an area thought to be in the south-west of Scotland, Ryderch Hen from the Strathclyde Britons and Guallauc from the Gododdin. There are other references to this battle in early Welsh poetry and Smyth makes the point that Morcant was 'an unidentified northern British leader' [1984, p.21] and that he later betrayed Urien. It is tempting to see Morcant as possibly representing a specifically Pictish power here, in that we can understand these leaders combining their tribal war-bands to try and thwart the rising power of the Northumbrians as their ancestors had combined against Agricola. This is unprovable, but the coming together of these leaders in such a fashion can be interpreted as still being essentially tribal. It is as the struggles against the rising power of Northumbria develop that I would suggest these separate, though related, tribal groupings begin to be forced into becoming more central-ised through the process of themselves having to be ready to resist the Northumbrians on a virtually permanent basis. This process might well be akin to Marsden's suggested methodology of the development of the Germanic war-band leader, the *cyning*, into a king through just such a process of militarisation. While this would not preclude the type of alliance that we see in operation at Lindisfarne it would go some way to providing a model for the development of the separate areas of these tribes into identifiable proto-kingdoms. I would therefore suggest on this model, that it is from around this period that we can begin to under-stand the changing use of the term Pict with it increasingly being applied exclusively to the more northern tribes, instead of the more generic usage of the Romans, with the Britons of Strathclyde and the Scots of Dalriada also becoming much more centralised and structured political entities themselves. Such a process could only be furthered by the increasing role within these societies of churchmen like Columba and though we have no documentary proof, the effects of a literate and aggressive Church on the advancement of such a process of centralisation is not difficult to imagine.

While the structure of the Columban Church was based around the idea of the *muinntir* or brotherhood, and each localised church was under the control of an abbot, as opposed to the more hierarchical bishop-led structure of the Roman Church, Columba's and later Adomnan's actions clearly show that they were heavily involved in the politics of their day. That Columba had also been involved directly in battle underlines the reality that the role of the Church was in no way humble or self-effacing and that the idea of the meek missionary going happily to martyrdom among the pagans is a selective reading of contemporary events.

Adomnan's intention was to present as positive a picture of Columba as possible and all the material derived from lives of early saints conforms to this approach. They are not an attempt to give what we nowadays consider as history.

This process of change from a tribal structure towards something more like the modern nation state was surely accelerated in the seventh century as the control of the Roman Church expanded after the Synod of Whitby in 664CE. As long as the Columban Church flourished, its localised control would have tended to keep it parallel to the tribal structure it accompanied, but the power of individuals such as Columba and later abbots perhaps itself suggests a weakening of the social structure of the tribes. Whether the function of this early Christian Church replaced an earlier role of druids or druidesses is unclear [McHardy 2003] but the introduction of literacy and the idea of an essential dogma at the core of religious belief and practice could not but have a profound effect on people whose belief system was previously based within their own environment. It meant that the essentially communal focus of tribal thought was replaced by something not only more abstract but also external to the community.

Other battles at this same period mentioned in the *Annals of Tigernach* are the battle of Leithrig fought by Aedan, Gabran's son in 591CE [Anderson 1990, p.94] and also:

> The slaughter of the sons of Aidan, namely Bran and Domangart
> and Eochaid Find and Arthur, in the battle of Circhend, in which
> Aidan was conquered.
>
> [*Ibid*, p.118]

It is noticeable that again Tigernach here does not use the term king and
the latter battle appears to have been fought within the Pictish province
of Circinn. The specificity of these Pictish provinces is no longer taken
for granted but the location of the battle here supports the notion that we
are now entering into the period where the Picts are seen to inhabit the
northern part of Scotland, as Circinn is generally accepted as referring
to the lands north of the Tay, Angus and the Mearns. Tigernach does
not however mention Picts here. While I have suggested that from the
Roman point of view, probably followed by early monkish commentators, the term Picts was a loose one covering all of the tribes of Scotland,
there is no suggestion that the Scots and the Picts were not different
tribes. However this battle follows another entry in Tigernach for the
year 583CE which Aedan fought in the Isle of Man, though some have
interpreted the battle as being fought in Manau, the lands round Clack-
mannan [*Ibid*, p.90]. Again following the idea of tribal activity these
various battles may have been no more than large raids, even if the
scribes who noted the events in Ireland perceived them differently. After
this in 603CE, Aedan is said in Tigernach to have been defeated in battle
by the Northumbrians under Ethelfrith at a place called Degastan, possibly the Dawston Burn in Liddesdale, and his death is noted five years
later. Interestingly in Fordun's *Scotichronicon*, a serious attempt at a history of Scotland composed in the 1440s, refers to this event thus:

> ... and while from day to day his (Aidan's) army employed its
> leisure in burning and spoiling, on one of the days king Aethelfrith
> with a massed army came upon the Scots, who were scattered in
> this manner for robbery through the villages and the fields, and
> conquered them, not without great slaughter of his men...
>
> [Watt 1989, III, p.116]

Shortly before this Tigernach does refer to Gartnait at his death in
601CE as king of the Picts, but the possibility exists that these battles
were still essentially following the practice of inter-tribal raiding where

loot was the primary objective. The actions of the Northumbrians in the coming decades were to change that.

That the battles between the new religion and old beliefs were still not settled is shown by the killing of Columba's rival Donnan in Eigg in 617CE [*Annals of Ulster*, URL 617.1] With the changing political situation arising from Northumbrian expansion and what appears to be an ongoing religious struggle these were troubled times for the Picts and all the peoples in southern Scotland. It is impossible to delineate precisely how and when tribalism was replaced by a more centralised social structure, but it is probable that this was a process that varied in its rate of progress in different parts of the country. Those areas furthest from the Northumbrians may well have held on to essentially tribal systems as was the case in the Highlands, but the changes happening in Dalriada, Strathclyde and Pictland must have had knock-on effects throughout their entire areas. However the essentially kinship nature of life for the majority of people is likely to have continued and positing the idea of a single leader with some level of power over all the Pictish peoples is not the same as suggesting the wholesale replacement of tribalism with something akin to the hierarchical and aristocratic structures of feudalism. The ties of blood that have been understood in the light of most interpretations of Scotland's past as pertaining essentially to dynasties, royal or aristocratic, were much more likely to have remained integrated into society as a whole in Pictish times. If, as is generally accepted, we must understand most of the First Millennium in terms of a series of interlinked tribal structures we must be very careful in using the term king. One term that crops up in several recent histories is tribal kingdom, an idea that is so amorphous as to be essentially meaningless. If we use the term king in relation to Pictish society in this period, and perhaps till considerably later, we have to realise that however the tribes of the Picts saw their supreme leader, it was not as a king as the term is now generally used. Having arisen from a purely tribal society the role of the Pictish kings must have reflected the ideas that held such a society together, particularly the central unifying importance of the kindred that was, to a large extent, an extended family. While there are undoubtedly gradations of status within tribal societies they are not reliant upon the rigid class differentiations of feudal-type societies where the king, and his court, are effectively above and over the rest of society.

One marker of the changing realities coincided with the slaughter of

Donnan and his companions in Eigg. According to Bede, Eanfrid son of Ethelfrith, who ruled Northumbria 593–616, went into exile when Edwin became king of Northumbria after himself being driven into exile by Ethelfrith. Bede presents Edwin as bringing Northumbria into the Church having set up a council of his leading men after which the pagan chief priest willingly destroyed his own altars [Bede 1955, p.124f]. Edwin is presented as a devout king and on his death Bede tells us:

> During the whole of Edwin's reign the sons of Ethelfrith, his predecessor, together with any young nobles who had lived in exile among the Scots or Picts, were instructed in the teachings of the Scottish (Columban) church, and received the grace of baptism. But on the death of their enemy Edwin, they received permission to return to their native land and Eanfrid, as eldest son, inherited the crown of Bernicia.
>
> [*Ibid*, p.138]

Remembering that the title of Bede's work is the *History of the English Church and People*, this passage perhaps tells us of more than the supposedly inexorable progress of Christianity under God's will. Here we have a contender for the kingship of the Northumbrians living among the northern tribes for a period around 16 years before going home to take over the leadership of his people. Most interpretations of this incident have seen Eanfrid as being made welcome at the court of King Nechton and staying on through the reigns of Cinoich and Garnard. As we shall see below, Eanfrith's presence amongst the Picts, rather than the Scots, as Smyth points out [1984, p.61], was to have far-reaching consequences in establishing the dominance of the Roman Church.

However, the problem with such interpretations is that they are based on the assumption that both Northumbria and Pictland were kingdoms with the full panoply of aristocratic support for their kings, provided through the assumed institution of a royal court. This has not been established and it is very unlikely that matters were so clear-cut amongst the Pictish peoples at this time. The inference by most commentators to date has been that Eanfrith and his companions were welcomed at a Pictish court as fellow aristocrats. Again this is based on assumptions about Pictish society that have never been truly tested, never mind proven. Even if the Picts were beginning to move away from an essentially tribal structure at this time, we still have no support for the idea of a truly royal court that would have in some unspecified manner welcomed Eanfrith and his companions as fellow aristocrats. What seems more likely is that they were welcomed as notable warriors and that whatever role the Pictish leader or leaders of the time had, they would have been aware of the possibility of future political benefit from welcoming Eanfrith. This hope would probably have been that after so many years amongst the Picts Eanfrith would have been able through his role as a Bernician leader to exercise some restraining influence on the Northumbrian king, Edwin, and prevent further incursions to the north. If this was indeed the hope, it was to prove ill-founded.

Within less than a handful of years the Northumbrians were again heading north. The *Annals of Tigernach* tell us that in 640 was

The battle of Glen Mairison, in which the people of Donald Brecc fled; and the siege of Etain.

[Anderson 1990, p.163]

This is mentioned two years earlier in the *Annals of Ulster* and while Anderson notes [*Ibid*, p.164] that there is some dubiety as to the precise location of Glen Mairison, he accepts, as is the general opinion, that the siege of Etain refers to Edinburgh. The possibility of the reference being to Glen Moriston on the shores of Loch Ness is worth considering in the light of some of the ideas concerning the Battle of Dunnichen in 685. Given that we know this is a period of Northumbrian expansion there is no reason to doubt that this was a Northumbrian campaign, possibly led by Oswald. It also tells us that Edinburgh, or at least the Castle Rock, was being defended against the southern incursion. This can only have been a Gododdin stronghold at this period and it is generally accepted that the Northumbrians were successful in their siege. In 642CE Tigernach tells us that Brude, son of Foith, died and though there is no specific mention as to how he met his death, given the troubled times it is at least possible that he died in battle, the most likely opponent being the Northumbrians.

However in the same year, according to various Annals, Domnall Brecc [Anderson 1990, p.167], said to be king of Dalriada was killed by Owen, king of the Britons of Strathclyde in a battle at Strathcarron. This serves to underline the political instability of the times and can be interpreted in more than one way. Was this battle a result of ongoing disruption between the Britons and the Scots that was rooted in their tribal past or was it the start of something new? The effects of Northumbrian expansion, which once might have led the Britons and Scots to unite, now, through the process of increasing centralisation within the two groups, makes it seem that those communities, or their leaders, were seeking to consolidate power by following the Northumbrian example, rather than relying on the tribal processes of the past. There is also the strong possibility that they were both intent on trying to gain power through the taking over of territory belonging to the tribes of the Gododdin who had apparently been overwhelmed by the Angles of Northumbria. Whatever the specific causes for this battle it would appear to be clear that the situation is moving beyond the normative behaviour of tribally structured societies and we are beginning to see political behaviour akin to that of nation states or kingdoms. In 642CE Oswald, as the over-king of Northumbria, is mentioned as having gone into battle against the Britons of Strathclyde. While none of these dates can be guaranteed they do point to the changes happening as the Angles constantly tested the strength of their neighbours to the north and west, and those changes were being forced on all of those neighbours; Britons, Scots and Picts.

Around this time the monastery of Abercorn on the southern shore of the Forth near South Queensferry was founded and Smyth sees this as an explicit political move on the part of the Northumbrians. He tells us

> Abercorn would have been founded as a frontier outpost to monitor the Picts and Britons of Manaw and beyond, and its new Anglian bishop would ensure the channelling of Northumbrian influence among the Pictish clergy and their aristocracy... We appear to be faced with a power struggle for the immediate control and occupation of the strategically crucial plain between Stirling and Edinburgh.
>
> [1984, pp.65–6]

While I would suggest it is still anachronistic to speak of a Pictish aristocracy at this time, this gives us a pretty clear picture of what was happening in contemporary society. The area around the Gap of Stirling in particular remained of major strategic importance up to the 18th century, and in the seventh century control of this area was vital for either advancing north into Pictish territory or, for the Picts and their allies, coming south. With what appears to be the collapse of Gododdin power following the siege of Etain the situation was undoubtedly fluid. Most commentators to date have seen this period as a time when one king or another dominated, Smyth suggesting that Neithon of Strathclyde in the 620s was the overlord of southern Pictland, by which he means the country between the Forth–Clyde line and the Mounth, the spur of the Grampians that juts out to near the coast at modern Stonehaven. As has been noted above, the southern Picts would seem in earlier times to have included the Britons and even the Scots whom Smyth sees as now dominating the Picts as a discrete and separate entity. I suggest we are seeing something much more fluid. As the effects of Northumbrian expansion were felt, the old social structures, with inter-tribal raiding between groups or tribes that could at other periods be allies, were beginning to weaken, particularly in those areas, like the southern Forth plain, which were of ongoing strategic importance. The fact that a warrior-based, Celtic-speaking society 'addicted to raiding' continued to exist for more than a millennium shows that whatever the extent of these changes they did not result in the total cessation of tribalism within the Pictish areas, nor probably among the Scots in Argyll. It is also from this period that the term southern Picts as used by most commentators on Scottish history begins to have any precision, though the precise relationship between southern and northern tribal groupings, particularly in the light of the late survival of tribal society, is anything but clear. It is also unclear how far Northumbrian control extended and just how extensive it was. It has been accepted by Smyth and others that when Bridei son of Foith died in the late 630s or early 640s, his successor was in some way under the domination of the Northumbrians. This is because he occurs in the Pictish King Lists as Talorcan, son of Eanfrith, presumed to be the Northumbrian who had lived amongst the Picts up until 634CE. This raises several questions which as yet have no answers.

How exactly did one man, no matter his dynastic claims, manage to ensure that an armed population – for that is what tribal society suggests – gave him loyalty and obedience? Apart from the survival of the Highland tribes with their warrior traditions there was also the continuance of the Wappenshaw tradition in the Lowlands into the late medieval period. These were the occasions when the local population was gathered together to show what weapons they possessed, illustrating that an armed populace was part of Scottish society for a very long time after this period – mainly due to the fact that invasion by the English was a constant fear. By claiming all men as warriors I am suggesting that all men had been trained as such and in times of need were capable of functioning as such, even if the war-band of the tribe would generally be drawn from the fittest of the younger men leavened by a core of experienced and skilled older warriors. Short of total occupation by an armed force such populations are virtually impossible to control, a particularly striking example of this being the military occupation of virtually every Highland glen and every city north of the Forth–Clyde axis, from Culloden in 1746 through to at least 1753 and possibly later [McHardy 2004, p.262ff].

So if Talorcan was a puppet king it seems likely that either he controlled a limited area of the country or there were a great many Northumbrian troops amongst the Picts. The idea that people united by bonds of kinship, which both define them and their history, can simply have their leader or leaders replaced at the behest of an outside authority does not hold water. The problems the Romans faced in a similar situation which earlier I have compared to the problems of the British Empire (and their recent successors) in Afghanistan, would apply equally to the Northumbrians – without either total military occupation or the eradication or displacement of the population and a widespread settlement of incomers, they would be unable to suppress and control local tribal warriors.

If there had been a devastating campaign it is possible that the native tribes had too few men to fight the invader, or had been scattered and found it difficult to resist. Again however given what we know of Scotland from the time of Mons Graupius, the capacity of the natives to utilise their raiding traditions in developing guerrilla tactics was considerable and did not disappear for another thousand years and more. Also as the recent re-assessment of Dalriada [Campbell 2000] has shown, what is passed on as history is not necessarily grounded in fact. Talorcan is said in the *Annals of Tigernach* [Anderson 1990, p.172] to have been successful in battle against the Scots in Strath Ethairt, but whether this was part of the ongoing battles between Picts and Scots which may have been little more than large-scale inter-tribal raiding, or some kind of campaign in support of long-term Northumbrian expansionism is unclear, but the reference shows that Talorcan was acting in a similar manner to other

Pictish 'kings', going into battle with the Scots. It is possible that some of the references to repeated battles between the Picts and Scots, if they were raids rather than anything more politically driven, would themselves lead to further raids, as reprisals, or perhaps even develop into blood feuds, always a possibility in essentially tribal societies. The Angles of Northumbria however were clearly driven by deliberate expansionism. The *Chronicle of Holyrood*, dating from the period of the late 12th to the early 13th centuries, tells us that in 655

> ... Oswiu... for the most part subdued the nations of the Picts and Scots, which hold the northern territories of Britain and made them tributary.
>
> [Anderson 1990, p.175]

This is quite explicit and while we cannot be sure of how much control the Northumbrians actually had in Pictish, or Scottish areas, it does underline the aggressive nature of Northumbrian politics towards their neighbours. Oswiu's role as king of the Northumbrians is clear and his expansionist policies had to rely on a centrally organised society that could support a permanent army, rather than occasional war-bands, raised to fulfill short term needs. Such aggression would have forced the Picts and the Scots to react along similar lines. The constant threat of attack would force the war or raiding band process to become something more regularised, in turn giving the leaders of such groups a more continuous role of authority.

CHAPTER SEVEN

From chief to king

THE MOST FASCINATING AND tantalising documents concerning the Picts are the Pictish King Lists [Anderson 1990]. These survive in a variety of different forms, none of which can be shown to be earlier than the 14th century and as Foster points out [1996, p.20], they are likely to suffer from both scribal error and political bias. Given their late date we can perhaps best see the lists as early medieval attempts to understand the past – meaning that it would be natural for whoever compiled them to think in terms of a society headed by a king, because that was how society then functioned. As they were compiled in this form so long after the times described, Molly Miller's suggestion [1979] that the King Lists cannot be seen as truly historical before the 660s – meaning that there are no other sources which can support them before that period – makes a great deal of sense. Talorcan, though slightly earlier than this, does appear to be historical, his reign generally accepted to have lasted for about four years in the mid 650s. Smyth's assertion that there was 'a major Pictish revolt' [1984, p.66] put down by Ecgfrith, the king of Northumbria, in 672CE seems impossible to substantiate. There is however little doubt of the growing power of Northumbria. This was not just a matter of battle but of attempted conquest.

It has already been suggested that the close involvement of Columba in Dalriadan politics effected the development of that society and the role of the Christian Church in the development of Northumbria is also significant. In the early 660s the priest Wilfrid became bishop of Ripon, part of the Northumbrian kingdom of Deira, replacing the previous incumbent who was a member of the Columban Church which still looked to Iona for spiritual leadership. The rest of Northumbria was still essentially Columban and thus organised round the figures of the abbots who were in charge of each monastery. The first Christian king of the Northumbrians had been Oswald, 634–41CE, who had apparently been Christianised while in exile among the Picts along with Eanfrith, who was king of the southern Northumbrians for a short while before Oswald came to power. Bishops within the Columban Church had limited powers and were under the command of the abbots. Wilfrid, though a North-umbrian, had spent time on the Continent at Rome and Lyon and had begun to follow the ways of the Continental Church. While this meant that the monks cut their hair differently from the Columban monks, there was also the problem of different dates for Easter, which was sup-posedly the main reason for Wilfrid organising the Synod of Whitby in 664, an event which brought in leading ecclesiastics from all over the British Isles. There is no doubt that the using of different calculations in the Roman and Columban Churches was causing problems, particularly in Northumbria. Bede tells us

> ...the confusion was such that Easter was kept twice in one year, so that the king (Oswiu) had ended Lent and was keeping Easter, the Queen and her attendants were still fasting and keeping Palm Sunday.
>
> [1955, p.182]

The upshot of the Synod was that Oswiu resolved to follow Roman practice and effectively began the disestablishment of the Columban Church from its traditional role. Though the apparent reason for this religious gathering was to address the problem of different dates for Easter, there appears to have been a hidden agenda. Smyth informs us that the result of the expulsion of Columbans was to 'allow Wilfrid to build his ecclesiastical empire on the ruins of the pillaged British church' [1984, p.27]. Here he is apparently referring to the Columban Church.

However it wasn't just Wilfrid gaining personally. Monasteries didn't just provide literate monks who could keep records, they tended to be the focus of a wide range of social and economic activities which made them increasingly important, and they were the natural centres of urban development along with royal courts, which were usually located near to important monasteries anyway. Their increasing role within Pictish society, and their part in changing it, would of course be assisted by the aforementioned Christian policy of taking over earlier sacred sites which had long been of fundamental importance to the local communities. Now with the control of them passing from the local provenance of the Ionan tradition to the control of Rome, the Church became more hierar-chic and could not help but be less responsive to their immediate local populations. And the Church based in far away Rome probably now became the owner of the church lands. The Columban Church with each institution under the control of its own abbot could function perfectly well alongside societies that were still in their main essentials, tribal. The Roman Church, looking far away for direction, broke this immediate and personal local link. This I suggest can only have accelerated the movement towards what we now think of as the nation state. The gathering of tithes, a 10th of people's produce, to support the Church was in itself the beginning of that most ubiquitous (and some would say iniquitous) of government activities, taxation, something which the Romans had instituted in England. Oswiu was turning his back on a system that had looked for leadership, in ecclesiastical matters at least, to an institution in the land of the Scots, and aligning himself with not only the Roman-following societies of southern England, but of Christian Europe. This directly affected the Picts as the immediate effect of this would appear to have made Oswiu and his successor Ecgfrith even more expansionist in their policies. The structure of the Roman Church, closely following that of the earlier Roman Empire could only accelerate the move away from ancient modes of behaviour based above all else around the ties of kinship.

Matrilineal succession

One of these oft-argued ancient modes of behaviour that continues to pose questions is the succession of the Pictish kings themselves. While, as noted, we cannot be sure of the precise historicity of them much before this period, the King Lists clearly show that the fathers of the kings, as given, were not only never kings themselves, but were frequently from external societies [with possibly in some cases the parent actually being the mother, see below]. In the earlier period the King Lists refer to, we cannot rule out the possibility that these external societies, particularly those of Dalriada and Strathclyde, were perceived as being, if not precisely Pictish themselves, at least close relations following the argument presented earlier. However by the period towards the end of the seventh century we see no change in this pattern – no son following his father as king – and if we accept the essentially tribal nature of most of Scotland up to this period then the existence of external fathers can itself be construed as little more than the continuation of ancient modes of behaviour, rooted in the tribal past.

The fact that no son succeeds his father has of course given support to the idea of matrilineal succession amongst the Picts and this idea has been reconsidered relatively recently. In a lecture to the Pictish Arts Society in November 2002, Dr Emily Lye of the School of Scottish Studies proposed a model of how this could have functioned. She suggested that there were two dominant female lines, one of which preserved the actual sovereignty of the land in the person of the queen who succeeded her mother, and to whom the candidate for king was married before himself taking office. The other line would have preserved a continuum of candidates for that marriage and would effectively be a line of King-mothers, with of course the usual reservations about the term king here. This actually resonates very strongly with my own analysis of what appears to be an underlying Mother Goddess concept in pre-Christian Scotland, centred on a dual mother goddess figure who was alternatively represented as winter, death, night etc and as a golden, fertile, life-giving goddess of Summer [McHardy 2003 *passim*, 2005 Chapters 2.12; 2006 Chapters 5, 8, 9]. That this duality can also be discerned in the pre-Christian symbols of the Pictish Class 1 stones will be considered in the forthcoming work on Pictish symbols. By the late seventh century this suggested system would have undergone substantial change because of the changing political situation and the role of providing the candidate for king appears to have been passed to groups external to the core Pictish society. This would not necessarily have altered the line of sovereignty within that core society. It is also the case that the idea of sovereignty being represented by a female is not unique to the Picts. Writing of a variety of Irish traditions, Rees and Rees tell us,

> The relation between Irish kings and their realm is often portrayed as a marriage, and the inauguration is often portrayed as a wedding-feast. The country is a woman, the spouse of a king... A union between the king and the goddess of the land was an essential part of royal ritual in ancient civilisations on the Near East...
>
> [1990, p.74]

So if the Picts did in fact have a matrilineal form of succession they were not that unusual. While such a system may have been rooted in the far past it does not make the Picts particularly mysterious or even enigmatic.

One specific aspect of the King Llists was examined by Kyle Gray. Here she points out that a considerable number of the names given as being the parent of the king are not necessarily male. She informs us

... acceptance of the theory that the 'progenitor side' names are mostly female would neatly and simply explain the mysteries of the King List that so puzzled Skene and his followers. No progenitors were kings themselves because – except for a few male foreigners who for lack of Pictish blood were not kingship material – they were women who by virtue of their gender could not be kings. And no son is listed as succeeding his father as king because fathers were not recorded.

[1996, p.12]

If, as I have posited, the Picts up to this period were still essentially tribal, such a continuance of a tradition, rooted in ancient pre-Christian practice is anything but impossible. That the King Lists were first written down by Christian monks is indisputable and their relevance is not necessarily limited to the period when their historicity is provable. The assumption that the 'natural' form of succession is primogeniture i.e. the first born male succeeds his father, might be true in Classical and Christian works but can hardly be thought the norm in Scotland, certainly before the period when our kings began aping the feudal manners of their southern peers. In the 11th century Malcolm Canmore was succeeded first by his own brother, then by his sons, one after the other. This is much more like the clan, i.e. tribal succession, where the person closest to the original founder is the natural successor, meaning that a brother of a chief should always be preferred to a son. It is important to realise that within kinship based societies where everyone is well aware of each other's attributes and limitations, the role of election, from among those entitled to be considered for a particular socio-political position, was always important. The interpretation of such societies by monks, raised within the Christian and Classically-based education system that brought its own external ideas along with new religious concepts and literacy itself, was neither inherently sympathetic nor possessed of a deep level of understanding. Their education came from ideas based upon societies that were hierarchical, literate and essentially urban. Tribal society in First Millennium Scotland was none of these.

We must further consider the influence of Irish politics on such texts as do survive in or about Scotland as delineated by Campbell:

> Recent research has highlighted how Middle Irish historians were promulgating a view of Irish kingship which had a considerable effect on Scottish politics from 10th to the 13th centuries. Herbert (2000) has shown how the Irish view of kingship, and political marriages, were influencing Scottish kings in the 10th century towards the concept of kingship of a land (Alba) rather than a people (the *Dal Riata*), and Duffy (2000) has demonstrated that there was Irish support for one line of rival claimants to the Scottish throne in the 11th century. This influence continued in the 12th–13th centuries (Broun 1999). It is probable that in this climate that the manipulation of the genealogies took place, with each lineage trying to outdo the other in stressing their antiquity and Irish origins.
>
> [2000, p.288]

That this influence was being perpetrated through the medium of scholastic monkish writing is clear. As we have no contemporary literary Pictish records we are constantly forced to deal with material that has to be treated carefully. The truism that history is written by winners might be better expressed as history is re-written by winners.

In the case of seventh century Britain as a whole, the clear winners were the Roman faction of the Christian Church. With the weakening of the power of the Columban Church the influence of Rome, and that of Classical education, could not but increase. As we shall see this was soon to have a specific effect on Pictish society.

CHAPTER EIGHT

Conflict and consolidation

IN 672CE THE *Annals of Tigernach* tell us that Drest, King of the Picts, was expelled from his kingdom [Anderson 1990, p.181]. Anderson interprets this as Drest being thrown out by his own people because he was essentially a puppet of Oswiu the king of Northumbria, but this is not explicit. Following the suggestion that earlier Talorcan had also been some kind of cats-paw of the Northumbrians, how would the relationship between Oswiu and Drest have worked out in practice? In fact the *Annals of Tigernach* may be giving us the answer. If indeed Drest was expelled by his own people, this would possibly be precisely because he was seen as not providing enough resistance against the Northumbrians. This not only follows tribal practice but is again something that can be seen as being particularly Scottish. As mentioned above, in the most famous document in Scotland's history, the Declaration of Arbroath, it is made explicitly clear that King Robert I will be replaced if he does not continue to resist English attempts to conquer Scotland. While this is 642 years in the future I suggest it underlines my contention that we are not dealing with a society based around the generally accepted ideas of kingship in which the king is supreme over society. The fact is that the declaration, a letter to the Pope sent on behalf of 'the whole community of the realm of Scotland', suggests that kingship was essentially perceived as being subordinate to the community of the nation as a whole. In this respect it is notable that Scottish kings, and queens, were kings and queens of Scots, not of Scotland. Such a belief must have been even stronger in the period when the Picts were only beginning to move from their tribal structures. The survival of tribal behaviour, or certainly local independence from the centralised kingship of Scotland, lasted till the 13th century in Galloway, in the Borders till the late 16th century and in the Highlands till the 18th century. This is clear evidence that kinship rather than kingship lay at the heart of much of Scottish society till long after the Picts merged with the Scots to form the basis of the nation of Scotland.

Drest was succeeded by Bridei son of Bile, who was to have a significant influence on the situation. Whether or not Talorcan (653–7),

Gartnait (657–663) or his brother Drest (663–671/2) could have been puppets of Northumbria and under the control of Oswiu (642–671) and his successor Ecgfrith (671–685) is anything but certain, but what is abundantly clear is that Northumbrian expansion continued throughout the period. From the siege of Edinburgh in the early 640s onwards the Northumbrians had had a great deal of success. The establishment of the monastery of Abercorn on the south bank of the Forth just east of modern South Queensferry, is reflective of what they must have perceived as conquest of the lands to the north. Bede says that during Oswiu's reign that he 'subjected the Picts to English rule' [1955, p.217].

When Ecgfrith succeeded Oswiu he too had turned to the north. This is from the *Life of Bishop Wilfrid*, quoted in Marsden:

> ... in his early years, while his kingdom was still weak the bestial tribes of the Picts felt a fierce contempt for their subjection to the Saxons and threatened to throw off the yoke of slavery: and they gathered together countless tribes from every nook and cranny in the north, like swarms of ants sweeping from their hills in summer... On hearing this King Ecgfrith, though humble among his own people and magnanimous towards his enemies, prepared a troop of cavalry at once... and with the help of the sub-king Beornheth, he attacked with his little band of God's people the vast and invisible forces of the enemy. And he slaughtered an immense number of their people, filling two rivers with the corpses, so that strange to relate, their slayers crossed the rivers with dry feet in pursuit of the crowd of fugitives; and their tribes, reduced to slavery, remained subject under the yoke of captivity until the day the king was slain.
>
> [1992, p.160]

This is presumably the incident that Smyth is referring to as 'the massacre of the Pictish army by Ecgfrith *c.*672CE, [1984, p.63]. There is a problem however in that there are no contemporary records to support this battle and the tone of the language is such as to make its propagandistic aspect abundantly clear. Not only are the Picts compared to insects, akin to Gildas 'the foul hordes of Scots and Picts, like dark throngs of worms who wriggle out of fissures in the rock when the sun is high and the weather grows warm' but the portrayal of the 'humble' and 'magnanimous'

Ecgfrith leading a small band of God-inspired Northumbrians against a vast horde of northern savages is difficult to take seriously. The existence of the Anglian monastery at Abercorn however does suggest that Northumbrian influence as far north as the Forth, and possibly further north, was a reality. Whatever the extent of Northumbrian control, the Picts were not conquered for good.

Anderson [1990, p.181] clearly refers to Drest as a Northumbrian vassal, an anachronistic term suggesting that he saw Pictish society as in some way feudal. There is no basis for this assumption but given Bridei's subsequent actions it must remain possible that Drest, like Talorcan and Gartnait, may have been under Northumbrian influence. Alternatively they may just not have proved sufficiently dedicated in resisting the Northumbrian incursions. The idea that Oswiu could have a leader of the Picts as a 'vassal' makes clear the problems we have in understanding the period. A vassal refers to someone who has accepted the authority of another in a specific fashion that includes military service. In terms of kings it means that the lesser king is effectively accepting that he is in a subordinate role and must obey his superior. While all of this undoubtedly happened, to varying extents, in countries where feudalism was established, the idea that seventh century Scotland functioned like this cannot be established and such evidence as we do have suggests that the basic tribal kinship structure of Pictish society, and likewise the polities of Strathclyde and Dalriada had not been replaced by anything remotely like feudalism. The Declaration of Arbroath in 1320 with its statement about replacing the king if he did not fulfill the needs of the nation tells us that even six and a half centuries later Scotland had still not become a truly feudal society.

Northumbrian society was a polity based on a centralised kingship, but to see it as feudal is likewise anachronistic. However the control that the Northumbrians achieved over large sections of south-eastern Scotland and possibly Fife could have had only dramatic effects on Pictish society. Just as the Northumbrians themselves had originally seen their society develop as a result of being full-time mercenary troops in the pay of Rome so the ongoing threat from Northumbria must have had a substantial effect on the structure of Pictish warrior society. The underlying tribal structure with its focus on inter-tribal raiding meant that each tribe would have had its own war-band. The persistent incursions from the south would have meant that such war-bands and their relationship with their leaders would have had to become more structured. Traditional inter-tribal raiding as it survived in the Highland areas was generally an activity that took place in the autumn, after the harvest had been gathered [McHardy 2004]. The war-, or raiding-, band, would have been drawn from the men-folk of the tribe whose labour was required during harvest to ensure that enough food was gathered and stored to survive the coming winter. Subsistence societies have first to feed themselves before any other activities can be contemplated and the southern Scottish term for the autumn moon, 'MacPherson's Lantern', so called because of repeated incursions by members of the MacPherson clan from far to the north, underlines the fact that cattle raiding was a relatively formalised activity happening at that specific time of the year. The need to counteract a permanent threat of invasion would have had an effect on how the warriors of such a society functioned. The role of the leader, and we should remember that in tribal societies the leader of such war-band activities would in most cases be the most talented strategist rather than a hereditary chief, would also take on a more permanent and thus important role. The requirement for what can be seen as a permanent command structure would necessitate a degree of centralisation amongst the scattered communities that itself would require further changes in society. While a war-band would be able to go raiding with sufficient food for perhaps a week or so – and as late Highland records tell us the clan warriors could survive on little more than oats and water for quite long periods – the very numbers involved in fighting off invaders would require greater organisation in food production and distribution. This in turn would have further effects on society in any extended period of threat from outside. The patterns developed in response to such stresses would in time become the norm themselves and alter the day-to-day life of tribal society. The role of the leader, whether we call him a king or a high-chief would become less social and more political in order to respond to ongoing problems caused by the necessity of constant, or almost constant warfare. The process of how the Northumbrian 'cynyngs' became kings can be seen as a model for this type of behavior. The central leader in this type of situation would require a command structure of trusted advisors and warriors around himself that would very easily develop into something akin to the courts of later kings.

There are several Annal entries for the 670s and one of them in 673 [Anderson 1990, p.182] refers to the burning of a monastery in Tiree.

There are no further details but it suggests the possibility that the Christianisation of the Picts perhaps had still not been completed, even after Columba's mission and the Synod of Whitby. Another confusing reference comes in 676 [*Ibid*, p.183], again in the *Annals of Ulster* where there is a reference to many Picts being drowned 'in Land-Abae', which is unclear. It is also unclear as to whether this is a reference to a natural disaster or some act of naval warfare. If it referred simply to something like a ship being lost at sea it would probably only have been mentioned if there was somebody of note on board, so it may be referring to something to do with battle. The *Annals of Tigernach* report in 678 that there was

> A slaughter of the tribe of Loarn in Tirinn [in a battle] between Ferchar Fotha and the Britons, who were the conquerors...
>
> [*Ibid*, p.184]

It is notable here that the reference is to the Cenel Loarn, one of the three Scottish tribes, rather than the Scots in general and there is no reference to Dalriada. This might suggest that even in this period when Northumbrian pressure appears to have been at its strongest, that inter-tribal raiding remained a regular aspect of everyday society in Scotland. 680CE sees the *Annals of Ulster* mention a siege of 'Dun-Baitte'. Anderson makes the point that an earlier commentator WF Skene suggested that this took place at Dunbeath in Caithness [*Ibid*, p.190]. There are however other possible locations and those involved are not mentioned. This event however may be linked to one the following year in the *Annals of Tigernach* where it says 'The Orkneys were destroyed by Bruide' [*Ibid*, p.191], an event also mentioned in the *Annals of Ulster*. This has been suggested as Bridei consolidating his power before taking on the power of Ecgfrith. If this is so then the possibility exists that a battle in Caithness could have been part of the same process. The Picts in Orkney, separated from the mainland, may well have been at least semi-independent or may have had a particular tradition of sea-born raiding in which case Bridei may have been ensuring that he would not be distracted from his main aim by raiding from the north. The following year, 683, there is a reference to sieges of both Dunadd in the Kilmartin valley and Dundurn at the east end of Loch Earn. Again these activities can be construed as Bridei making sure that he would have no distractions when he fought the Angles, though there is no mention of either personal names or of either Picts or Scots. Dunadd however was effectively the capital of Dalriada and Dundurn may well have been a Scottish stronghold on the edge of Pictish territory at the time. Alternatively the Picts may have laid siege to Dunadd and the Scots attacked Dundurn, which would make it part of Pictland. While the situation may never be clear, though extensive archaeological investigation of such indigenous sites would help, the overall picture is of widespread conflict along the borders of Pictland at least.

All of this leads up to one of the more famous battles of Scotland's history. Reported in various Annals and by Bede, this was the Battle of Dunnichen in 685 CE.

Bede's account tells us:

> King Egfrid, ignoring the advice of his friends and in particular that of Cuthbert, of blessed memory, who had recently been made bishop, rashly led an army to ravage the province of the Picts. The enemy pretended to retreat and lured the king into narrow mountain passes, where he was killed with the greater part of his forces on the twentieth of May in his fortieth year and the fifteenth of his reign...
>
> Henceforward the hope and strength of the English realm began to waver and decline, for the Picts recovered their own lands that had been occupied by the English, while the Scots living in Britain and a proportion of the Britons themselves regained their freedom... Many of the English at this time, were killed, enslaved, or forced to flee from Pictish territory. Among them the most reverend man, the bishop Trumwin, who had been appointed their bishop, withdrew with his people from the monastery of Abercornig which was situated in English territory, but stood close to the forth that divides the land of the English and those of the Picts.
>
> [1955, pp.252–3]

This was clearly a major victory for the Picts, enabling both the Scots in Dalriada and the Britons in Strathclyde to throw off the influence of the Northumbrians. The retreat of Trumwine from Abercorn on the south shores of the Forth suggests that Bede was possibly overstating the case when he says that the Forth divided the lands to the English from those of the Picts. Trumwine went all the way back to Whitby in Yorkshire and it is notable that there were ongoing battles between the Angles and the northern peoples in Lothian over the ensuing few centuries. Northumbrian control was almost certainly not as complete as Bede suggests. If the Angles held on to this part of Scotland why did Trumwine retreat so far to the south? Surely if he felt threatened on the banks of the Forth he could have chosen somewhere more safe in all the lands between Abercorn and the Tyne. We should remember that Bede was not only a Christian monk, but an Angle himself and it may be that here he was stating what had been the situation rather than what it was as he wrote. The idea that the P-Celtic speaking people of south-west Scotland, who less than a century before had created one of the great literary works of these islands in *Y Gododdin*, had been eradicated or that Anglian settlement had arrived in such numbers as to eradicate them is not really very likely. The concentration of Scottish historians on the supposed actions of kings has ignored what does appear to be the reality of the societies that were extant at the period. Perhaps the Northumbrians had completely uprooted the tribal societies of the Gododdin and their neighbours, replacing it with something new, but there is no specific evidence for this.

Yet again the dearth of indigenous early literary material has led to a situation where not only is the picture unclear, but it has been filled with assumptions that are essentially anachronistic. The existence of a Northumbrian created monastery at Abercorn on the Forth, even combined with the siege, and assumed taking of *Dun Etain* on Edinburgh Castle Rock, is hardly proof of either total subjugation of the Gododdin, or takeover and settlement by an Anglian population. Bridei's stunning victory quite possibly resulted in at least some of the areas to the south of the Forth reverting to the social and political habits of their tribal past.

For the Picts, and by now the term should be understood as referring to the peoples north of the Forth–Clyde line, the victory ensured their survival. The retreat from Abercorn does however raise several questions. Were the Picts still following the Columban Church practices? Would they have considered the Trumwine's establishment as a provocation? And also how much influence did the Angles actually have within any of the parts of Scotland they were supposedly in control of? There is no suggestion in this period that the two branches of Christianity, the Columban and the Roman, were actually at war with each other so why move so far from the Forth? The reality may well be that the extent of Northumbrian defeat was such that they were forced to retreat well beyond the southern banks of the Forth and that the Lothians may have reverted to more localised control, i.e. a return to a tribal based society. Alternatively we cannot rule out the possibility of some degree of Pictish control over some of these lands.

There is no doubt that Dunnichen, referred to by most English chroniclers as Nechtansmere, was a major turning point. Never again did the Northumbrians appear likely to conquer and subdue the northern peoples though battles continued for many years yet. Many commentators have seen Dunnichen as the point at which the future development of Scotland as a nation was ensured.

To date most commentators have accepted that the Battle of Dunnichen, Nechtansmere, or Linn Garan, the Pool of the Heron, as it appears in Irish sources, was fought near the tiny village of Dunnichen, about three miles east of Forfar in Strathmore. This part of the world has been understood as being part of the Pictish province of Circinn. The identification of the battle site rests partially on the place-name itself, Dunnichen deriving from Dun Nechtain, dun here taken as meaning hill-fort, but also on a particular Pictish symbol stone, now known as the Aberlemno Kirkyard Stone which, according to Cruikshank, 'depicts a battle-scene unique in the field of Pictish Art' [1991, p.23]. There is also a Pictish symbol stone which used to stand close to the suggested battle site, currently in Dundee Museum, but which does not appear to refer to the battle in any way we can now discern, none of its symbols having any understandable military reference. The archaeologist Craig Cessford suggested that the creation of the Aberlemno Kirkyard Stone may well have been based on a poem or saga about the battle itself, along the lines of the *Gododdin* [1996]. While it seems extremely likely that such a significant battle would have led to the creation of such a piece of heroic verse – remembering that even long after the arrival of Christianity literacy was extremely restricted and the majority of the population would still be living within an essentially oral tradition – this is unprovable. No one has, as far as I am aware, suggested that the stone in Aberlemno kirkyard is directly contemporaneous with the battle – the general opinion, based on art historical evidence, seeing it as eighth century – but Cessford's suggestion does not necessarily support the location near Forfar. A poem or ballad celebrating the battle that effectively saved the

Picts from conquest by the Northumbrians would have undoubtedly enjoyed wide provenance and there is a lack of any nearby archaeological support for the battle – there are no reports of any weapons or other artefacts being discovered when Dunnichen Moss was drained in the 18th century – but there is a further problem. Bede tells us that Ecgfrith was lured into 'narrow mountain passes'. The hills around Dunnichen are in fact not very high and have somewhat gentle slopes. Dunnichen Hill is just over 230 metres high and there is a flat area of about three kilometers wide between it and the hill to the south-east, Fothringham Hill, which is only slightly higher. It is through this gap that it has been suggested the Northumbrians arrived at the battle-scene. It is definitely not a narrow mountain pass. Again however we must be aware that Bede is not giving us an eye-witness account.

Alex Woolf has examined an alternative location for the battle which has long been considered a possibility. This is Dunachton on the shores of Loch Insh five miles north-east of Kingussie in Strathspey. Woolf tells us

> It is clear that this 'Dun Nechtain' is indeed a narrow place surrounded by inaccessible mountains and adjacent to a substantial loch. It is also at a strategically very important position at a point where as many as five passes through the mountains converge, Professor Barrow has pointed out that Ruthven Castle, some four miles to the south-west of Dunachton lay at the point where the three main passes out of Atholl... converge. To these can be added the two great water routes up into Badenoch from the south-west, along Loch Laggan and Loch Ericht. If we take Bede's claim that all Ecgfrith's friends thought him foolish to attempt such an expedition, then an adventure across the spine of Britain would seem to fit the bill better than a raid into the eastern lowlands...
>
> [Woolf 2006, p.188]

To get to this part of the world Ecgfrith's army would have had to come up through the pass of Drummochter which is indeed a high and narrow mountain pass and the location of Dunachton would give certain advantages. The passes through the mountains would provide ideal cover for the movement of troops unseen by an army approaching from the south. In passing, the mention of the water routes may also be significant.

Recent work such as Professor Cunliffe's *Facing the Ocean* have shown the important role of water transport in the far past and while he concentrated on coastal and ocean travel the case is just as strong for river and loch transport. With heavy wood cover and before widespread drainage, much of Scotland would have been boggy and difficult to cross. Water transport would always provide a viable alternative and we should be aware that the Picts probably used such transport on a regular basis. If it was fought in the north, some of the troops used in the Battle of Dunnichen could have arrived in the area by boats, probably made of skin, via the aforementioned lochs.

However Woolf does not only suggest that the Battle of Dunnichen took place far to the north of Forfar, he makes a further very salient point. The Pictish king – and if the interpretation of this battle as the result of a highly organised and widespread plan to draw the Northumbrian army into a well planned ambush is accepted, we are clearly looking at level of organisation throughout Pictish lands that would require an overall leader, who while in no way similar to a feudal king, would have considerable power – is said to have been Bridei mac Bile. In the *Annals of Tigernach* he is called the king of Fortriu. This is one of the names given as being a Pictish province in a 12th century document *De Situ Albanie*, that describes Scotland. The document says that Pictland was divided into seven provinces, Angus with the Mearns, Atholl and Gowrie, Strathearn with Menteith, Fife with Fothriff, Mar with Buchan, Moray and Ross, and Caithness. Another list from the same source describes these divisions as applying to the lands from the rivers Forth to Tay, from Tay to the Dee, from the Dee to the Spey, from the Spey to Drumalbin, Moray and Ross and Argyll. It is clear that these two lists do not coincide exactly but it has been long accepted that Fortriu must apply to the lands of Strathearn. This would mean that Bridei as king, or chief of that area, could have been fighting in the southern part of Pictland, in the province of Circinn, which appears to have been the later county of Angus which includes Dunnichen. The names of the provinces derive from another list in the Poppleton Manuscript which gives a supposed history of the Picts as descended from an original Cruithne – the name used for the Picts by Q-Celtic speakers – and the seven provinces are said to have been named for his seven sons Circinn, Fotla, Fortriu, Fib, Ce, Fidaid and Cat. These have been seen as referring respectively to Angus and the Mearns, Atholl and Gowrie, Strathearn and

Mentieith, Fife, Mar and Buchan, Moray and Ross and lastly Caithness. Woolf suggests otherwise, certainly in the case of Fortriu. He goes so far as to tell us that '... the map of the Pictish provinces which appears in almost every textbook is a doubtful construct of recent origin' [*Ibid*, p.191]. The story of Cruithne and his seven sons comes from an Irish manuscript attrributed to the Irish Nennius [Anderson 1990, p.xcxvii]. This links the origin of the Picts to the mythical Partholon in Irish tradition and seems to have the clear political motive of presenting Pictland as a unified and ancient state that preceded the formation of Scotland – something which I suggest could still have been anachronistic up to the time of the Battle of Dunnichen. I would further suggest that in fact this battle was one of the major steps along the road towards a unified state of some kind, but that at this time the Picts were still effectively a tribal society.

Woolf goes on to argue that Fortriu was not only in the north, probably Morayshire, but that the name preserves a link with the much earlier term Verturiones, one of the tribes of the Caledonians mentioned by Ptolemy. Like most commentators however he seems to have missed the reality that from the Roman perspective the Caledonians or Picts encompassed all of the tribes living north of Hadrian's Wall. However his argument about Fortriu being in the north has much to recommend it and it is worth noting that even as late as the 11th century Macbeth's power was rooted in this part of the country, and that even later, in the early 12th century, David 1 enforced a wholesale re-settlement of this part of the country, precisely because it was so difficult to control from further south. The area certainly appears to have been one of the ongoing power bases within Pictish society.

Bede's statement that the Scots and the Britons 'regained their freedom' does not say Dalriada and Strathclyde. We can be certain the Scots were in Argyll, but both the inhabitants of Strathclyde and the Gododdin were Britons. The new king of the Northumbrians was Aldfrith and over the next decade, he was visited by Adomnan, Abbot of Iona and writer of the *Life of Columba*, at least twice. The Picts under Bridei seem to have continued to follow the practices of the Columban Church, despite the decisions of the Synod of Whitby back in 664. This can hardly be considered surprising as the Roman Church may well have appeared to Bridei and his kin as playing an active part in the policy of Northumbrian expansionism. Adomnan was effectively the head of the Church in Dalriada and had accepted the decision of the Synod of Whitby and thus was following the tenets of the Church of Rome. While visiting Northumbria in the 690s Adomnan met Bede, who was in his 20s at the time. Bede tells us that when Adomnan came south

> He was earnestly advised by many who were more learned than himself not to presume to act contrary to the universal customs of the church, whether in the keeping of Easter or in many other observances, seeing that his following was very small and situated in a remote corner of the world. As a result he changed his opinions, and readily adopted what he saw and heard in the English churches in place of the customs of his own people. For he was a wise and worldly man, excellently grounded in knowledge of the Scriptures.
>
> [Shelley Price 1955, p.294]

This is a remarkable passage for what it says, and what it doesn't say. Firstly, though Adomnan was wise and excellently grounded in the Scriptures, there were according to Bede many more learned than him in Northumbria. The statement that his following was small and in a remote corner of the world is striking. A cleric writing in Northumbria was referring to Dalriada and Pictland, where as far as we can tell the Columban ways were still dominant, as 'a remote corner of the world'. This speaks of an unconscious arrogance in which the role of the Christian Church, as defined in Rome appears to have been following in the steps of the Roman Empire and effectively seeing itself as the benchmark for human thought and behaviour. It was this 'small following' that had been the cause of Northumbrians converting to Christianity in the first place with the arrival of Aedan in 635CE. What was left out is also of some importance. One of the realities that accompanied the shifts in devotional practice was that the ownership of the land belonging to the Church had to change. Abbots such as Adomnan were effectively leaders of individual churches living alongside the still essentially tribal population. Even if such abbots had absolute control over the lands allocated for supporting the church they were still essentially functioning within contemporary local society. Now the ownership of such lands was based in a vast organisation being run from Rome. This is a fundamental change and was one which gave considerable power to the leading bishops. It also meant that these bishops who were part of a vast bureaucratic machine, and as their monasteries were the centres of contemporary literacy and learning, had a growing influence on contemporary society and this can have had no other effect than to increase the centralising tendencies that were already under way. This soon had an effect among the Picts as we shall see. Adomnan's decision to follow the Roman ways caused a schism in the Columban Church according to Bede, with the monks in Iona refusing to change their practices. However the days of the Columban Church's power and influence were effectively over.

Smyth suggests [1984, p.136] that Adomnan and Bridei son of Bile were friends. Bridei is said to have been buried on Iona, which became for long after the normal practice of Scottish kings. Whether or not this suggests friendship between the two existed, it does underline the fact the Bridei was beginning to act more and more like what we would expect of a king – leading the massed tribes against the Northumbrians and after death being buried on Iona in a kingly fashion – rather than just some sort of war-band leader for the Picts. And Adomnan's general attitude towards both the Picts and Scots is not exactly kindly. In the *Life of Columba* he says

> And although neither of these nations was free from those grievous crimes which generally provoke the anger of the eternal Judge, yet both have been hitherto patiently borne with and mercifully spared. Now, to what other person can this favour granted them by God be attributed unless to St Columba, whose monasteries lie within the territories of both these people, and have been regarded by both with the greatest respect up to the present time.
>
> [Adomnan URL]

Is this simply a powerful cleric complaining because these recalcitrants will not follow his bidding and follow the dictates of Rome? Or were there perhaps deeper 'sins'? We cannot now know, but this passage shows just how careful we must be in interpreting the past through the eyes of those whose fundamental motivation was provided by their own religious beliefs.

In the year 693CE there is a reference in the *Annals of Ulster* [Anderson 1990, p.201] to a siege at Dunnottar just south of Stonehaven. Nowadays the great promontory there is dominated by the ruins of a massive medieval castle but even back at the end of the seventh century the site would have provided an easily defended site. In the light of what we know of Bridei's behaviour it is worth considering whether this was an instance of him consolidating his centralised rule. Sadly the Annal reference refers only to the siege, not by whom it was carried out. In the aftermath of a great victory against the invaders from the south who had long been dominant such a process would make sense. By beating the Northumbrians Bridei had shown both his worth and his power and it would make sense for him to consolidate his rule and it may have involved him subjugating specific tribes or areas.

Bridei died soon after this and it would appear that he left a Pictish society that was much more secure, and possibly more politically structured and centralised, than that he had inherited. The Northumbrians had been defeated and never again would they threaten the very existence of the Picts.

Bridei was succeeded by Taran according to the King List and he in turn was succeeded by Bridei son of Derile in 697CE. In 698CE there are references to Beorht the ealdorman being killed by the Picts, the *Annals of Tigernach* stating that it was in a battle between 'the Saxons and the Picts', Saxons here referring to the Northumbrians. Beorht was the son of Beornhaeth who was one of Ecgfrith's leading warriors and it appears likely that he had been killed at Dunnichen alongside his king. Marsden makes the point that warriors such as Beornhaeth would give up their lives 'in accordance with the warrior's ancient creed of loyalty to the royal "ring-giver" even until death in the blood-fray' [1992, p.203]. This is more than likely but such loyalty had little or nothing to do with the royalty or otherwise of a ring-giver, as it is a noted fact that amongst the surviving tribal warriors of the Highland clans that men would willingly die in battle to protect their chief, as head of their kin-group. The fact that this is the ancient warrior's creed is true, the relevance of royalty, minimal. There is no reference to where the battle when Beorht died took place, so we cannot tell if it was another surge of Northumbrian expansionism or a Pictish raid south. Marsden sees Beorht as being a sort of warden on the Pictish frontier [*Ibid*] and assumes that this was somewhere on the southern shores of the Forth but again we have no real proof to substantiate this. Even in the aftermath of the great battle at Dunnichen the struggles between Northumbrian and Pict were to continue and this would likely have led to Bridei mac Bile's successors having to continue and possibly expand the process of organisation that the situation necessitated.

In 704 Adomnan died but the Annals also tell us that there was 'a slaughter of the men of Dalriata, in the valley of the Leven' [Anderson 1990, p.208]. Again there is only this bald statement but given it is the men of Dalriada rather than any of the tribal groupings and the location of the battle at the southern end of Loch Lomond, this may well have been a battle between the Scots and either the Picts or the Strathclyde Britons whose capital Dumbarton sits at the junction of the rivers Leven and the Clyde. Whoever was involved it does show the ongoing fluidity of the contemporary political situation. Northumbrian power was on the wane and there may well have been a consequent power struggle between the different peoples of Scotland. Within two years of this event Bridei son of Derile died and he was succeeded by his brother Nechtan. Kyle Gray has pointed out that there are good grounds for considering Derile to have been a female name [Gray 1996, p.10]. As has been noted the society of the Picts was rooted in the far past but at this point we are in a situation of major change, mainly being forced by the twin stresses of external invasion and a politically, and territorially, expanding Church. Given that the Columban Church seems to have been closely intertwined with the local tribal communities it can be understood as at least partially continuing earlier sacral practice but the heirarchical structure and explicit rules of the Christian Church run from Rome could not but have an effect on those societies where it became the dominant model for religious behaviour.

Under the rule of Nechtan son of Derile (706–724), or certainly during the period he is said to have been the leading figure in Pictish society, there are further indications that society was changing. In 711CE the Northumbrians appear to have once more been trying to expand to the north. The *Annals of Tigernach* report a slaughter of the Picts in 'the plain of Mano'. This would appear to be the area also known as Manau Gododdin, which corresponds to the countryside long known as Clackmannanshire, on the north bank of the river Forth below Stirling. The *Anglo-Saxon Chronicle*, putting the battle in the previous year, says that the Northumbrians were led by Beorhtfrith, son of that Beorht who had been killed by the Picts in 698CE, and grandson of Beornhaeth who had probably died at Dunnichen [Savage 1984, p.89]. This entry however locates the battle between the rivers Carron and Avon on the south side of the Forth, which reinforces the idea that Manau covered both sides of the river. The precise meaning of Manau Gododdin is unclear but suggests that whichever tribe lived in this area were connected to the Gododdin to the east, who possibly had some sort of resurgence in the period immediately following Dunnichen. It is also in this part of the country that we have Camelon, one of the suggested locations for the possibly historical battle of Camlaan between Arthur and Mordred in the sixth century. Maclean sees this battle of 711 as of considerable significance. He writes:

> The Berhtfrith who supported the Romanising Wilfrid was apparently the ealdorman who defeated the Picts which suggests two possibilities for the Picts. First, Berhtfrith may have been in a position to dictate terms after his victory over the Picts in 711, although there is no indication that it was Nechtan whom Berhtfrith defeated. The annals merely record the death in the battle of 711 of Finnguine son of Deleroith, of whom nothing else is known. On the other hand, if the Picts whom Berhtfrith defeated were in rebellion against, or acting independently of Nechtan, the king may have welcomed the opportunity to consolidate his control of Pictland with Northumbrian help. In either case, Nechtan's ecclesiastical rapprochement with Northumbria led to peace between the two kingdoms, which lasted until the early years of the reign of Oengus son of Fergus.
>
> [Maclean 1998, p.183]

There is of course a third possibility here which Maclean hints at in his reference to Picts 'acting independently' of Nechtan. The very Romanisation to which Maclean refers can be seen as Nechtan acting in a more kingly manner, or at least trying to, and given the underlying inter-raiding traditions of the tribal Picts it is perhaps the case here that the Picts 'acting independently' were nothing other than a raiding band, or an extended version thereof, from a tribe other than that to which Nechtan belonged, or even that this was an instance of some of the Picts being dissatisfied with Nechtan and refusing to accept his leadership. Again the assumption here that we are dealing with a highly organised and structured society is not necessarily the case. If as I suggest, the process of moving from what was essentially a confederation of different tribal groupings to a more centralised state or kingdom took place over a considerable length of time, there are likely to have been instances where royal authority, or the attempt to create it, would have been resisted.

The same year a further battle between the Britons and Scots is reported in which the Scots proved victorious. Over the next few years there are various battles mentioned in the lands of the Dalriadans where the leader of the Cenel Loairn, Selbach mac Ferchair, was apparently fighting against the Cenel nGabrain. This suggests that Selbach, who is given as king of Dalriada in various sources, had to fight to defend his position. Whether this was part of ongoing internal problems or a result of the chaotic times is as yet unclear. In 713CE the *Annals of Tigernach* tells us that 'Talorc, Drostan's son was bound by his brother, king Nechtan.' 'Brother' here was suggested by Anderson [1990, p.214] to mean either brother-in-law or cousin, but this does not have to be the case. If Derile as suggested above was the mother of Bridei and Nechtan, their father may well have been Drostan which would make Drostan Nechtan's true brother. Again this suggests that the political situation remained fluid and that both Selbach and Nechtan were being forced to defend their positions against rival candidates from among their own kin-group. Into this situation stepped another important religious figure.

This was Egbert, an Anglian bishop who according to Bede arrived on Iona in 716CE and through his teaching

... the monks of Iona under Abbot Dunchad adopted Catholic ways of life about 80 years after they had sent to preach to the English nation.

[Shelley Price 1955, p.322]

Aedan had gone from Iona to Northumbria in the 630s at the behest of King Oswald, who had been baptised and wanted his people to renounce their old religion in favour of Christianity. Now we have the power of the Columban Church who had introduced Christianity being superceded by the Rome-based Church, through someone making the opposite journey. This I suggest is clear evidence of the organisation and efficiency of the Catholic Church in pushing its own agenda and this in turn can be seen as an important factor in the development of the tribal peoples towards a form of political rule that was moving from kinship towards kingship. Adomnan had earlier seen what has always been presented as the inevitability of this development, but we should keep in mind that all of the commentators on whom we are forced to rely for this period were of the Catholic persuasion. The existence of a highly structured organisation within the community that owed its allegiance to a body external to that community could only further a more structured and therefore heirarchic structure within that community, though this might well have been most obvious around the king and, at least initially, have little effect beyond his immediate circle. The survival of tribal life in small communities in the Highland areas for another millennium makes it obvious that such changes could not have had an immediate significant effect on all of the Picts. It is also true that the majority of the population of Lowland Scotland continued to live in similar small communities till the 17th and 18th centuries. The system of supporting churches which grew into the tithe system, where people gave a 10th of their produce to the church – and later its equivalent in money – would have provided a model for the raising of funds by lay leaders of society, whether we think of them as kings or as something more akin to a high-chief. Much of the confusion regarding these leaders comes from accepting what are essentially ideas from England's past and applying them to Scotland. The Declaration of Arbroath, noted above, shows that not only was the system of kingship different in Scotland into the Middle Ages but that its roots were grounded in the community at large in ways that were alien to the English crown. Up until the time of James I and VI the kings of Scots spoke the same language, Scots, as most of the population at large, something that had not always been the case in England, where the language of the court was French, and that of the people English. There is also ample evidence that the Scottish kings were much more approachable by the population than their southern counterparts.

However the leaders of the Picts in this period are certainly functioning differently from mere tribal chiefs. The year after Egbert persuaded the monks of Iona to abandon their traditional form of Christianity, Nechtan is reported as having made a significant decision. The *Annals of Tigernach* puts it baldly that there was an 'Expulsion of the community of Iona across the ridge of Britain by Nechtan' [Anderson 1990, p.217]. By so doing and thus accepting the Catholic Church he was taking on a lot more than just a new way of calculating Easter and having the monks wear a different hair-style. The heirarchic and structured functioning of the Catholic Church and its acquisition of property could not but provide a model for further change among the Picts. As for the Columbans, they continued to survive as small groups of what became known as Culdees in various locations like St Andrews and Dunblane, providing a parallel form of Christian worship for those who did not wish to desert the old ways, but from now on they had no real influence at all.

Nechtan's motives may well have had to do with the changing political scene. He was no doubt aware of the influence of the Roman form of Christianity after the Synod of Whitby, and after all Adomnan himself had accepted the new changes. It may be that he, more likely in conjunction with a group of advisors, thought it would be a wise move to accept this growing power. Apart from anything else the settling of religious differences and the subsequent probable increase in communications between the priesthood, could be of some assistance against further incursions. At the least it would appear that this coming together of religious practice might help control Anglian aggression and the further possibility of some level of intelligence becoming available through such increased communications would be something worthwhile.

Nechtan's reign continued for seven or so years after the expulsion of the Columban Church and it seems that within a couple of years the majority of the monks on Iona accepted the new form of Christianity through the influence of Egbert.

CHAPTER NINE

Into Alba

AT THE END OF HIS *History of the English Church and People,* Bede gives us a snapshot of the current state of Britain. This is thought to have been written somewhere between 725 and 731CE. It is interesting for several reasons:

> At the present time, the Picts have a treaty of peace with the English, and are glad to be united in Catholic peace and truth to the universal Church. The Scots who are living in Britain are content with their own territories, and do not contemplate any raids or stratagems against the English. The Britons for the most part have a national hatred for the English, and uphold their own bad customs against the true Easter of the Catholic Church; however they are opposed by the power of God and man alike, and are powerless to obtain what they want. For although they have a certain measure of self-government they have also been brought to some extent under the subjection of the English.
>
> As peace and prosperity prevail in these days, many of the Northumbrians, both noble and simple, together with their children, have laid aside their weapons, preferring to receive the tonsure and take monastic vows rather than study the arts of war.
>
> [1955, pp.324–5]

This is quite a picture. It is not borne out by the contemporary sources that we have. The various Annals surviving from this period show a period of widespread disorder, yet Bede would have us believe that the situation was such that the Northumbrians were living in a time of peace so secure that there was what appears to have been a massive religious movement within their society. The comment that the various classes of Northumbrian society preferred to become monks rather than study the arts of war does perhaps give a fitting conclusion to his book, which, it is believed, was finished around 731CE, just four years before his death. However his suggestion that the Britons are upholding their own bad customs tells us that the supremacy of the Catholic form of worship was not yet universal. His statement that his fellow Christians are opposed by the power of God underlines the animosity of the struggle between the different aspects of the same religion and this may well have played some part in the volatile situation described in the Annals, and some of the churches may well have been continuing to follow the old ways of the Columban Church.

He is definite about a treaty having been signed between the Angles and the Picts, a process that would surely have depended on the involvement of churchmen on both sides, the only section of society who we can be sure were literate at this time. It is possible that some lay people could read and write but there is no evidence to suggest this was widespread. The underlying reality of the situation Bede describes may simply be that Northumbrian policy in the period, due to their having suffered some significant reverses, was no longer as aggressively expansionist as it had been.

The situation amongst the Picts, and in Dalriada, was somewhat different. In the west the Annals tell us of several battles amongst the Scots between 717 and 721CE, in which Selbach of the Cenel Loairn fought and killed his own brother Ainfcellach [Anderson 1990, p.218] and went unsuccessfully into battle against Donald Becc of the Cenel Gabhran [Ibid, p.219]. There is an entry in the Annals of Tigernach for 723CE that tells us of 'The entrance into monastic life of Selbach, king of Dalriata' [Ibid, p.220]. He is not the only leader in this period to go into a monastery, and it is surely of some importance that he did not stay there, being mentioned in 727CE as having fought a battle against Eochaidh, son of Eochaidh, king of Dalriada. The situation amongst the Picts was equally complex.

Nechtan, who had been king of the Picts since 706CE, followed Selbach's example and went into a monastery in 724CE [Ibid, p.221]. Like Selbach he did not stay there long, for we read of him as 'being bound' by his successor Drust in 726CE. Had he gone into the monastery to find sanctuary, or was he using this period to gather his strength for an attempt to regain overall control? We cannot be sure but in the next few years there is apparently a political struggle for control going on in Pictland. The fact that Selbach behaved similarly in the same period suggests that they may well have been taking advantage of the respective monasteries to further their long-term political positions. The Annals of

Tigernach tell us that in the same year as Nechtan was 'bound', which surely must mean he was imprisoned by Drest, Drest was overthrown by Alpin, the son of Eochaid, presumably the Eochaid who was king of Dalriada from 695–7. According to one version of the Pictish King List Drest and Alpin reigned together [*Ibid*, p.cxxv]. No parentage is given for either Drest or Alpin and Nechtan is said to be back in charge by 728 or 729CE, having obviously left the monastery. It is possible that Alpin was fighting on behalf of Nechtan, or possibly the kin-group or tribe of which Nechtan was head.

The battles between what appears to be the different candidates for the leadership of the Picts at this period, were summed up by Smyth [1990, p.74] thus; in 726CE Drest defeats Nechtan and then Alpin defeats Drest; in 727CE Angus defeats Drest on three occasions; in 728CE Angus defeats Alpin who is then also defeated by Nechtan who has clearly left the monastery to re-enter the fray; in 729CE Angus defeats Nechtan then kills Drest in battle, thus ensuring his own position as king. These are the entries as given in the *Annals of Ulster*:

entry U726.1
Nectan son of Derile is imprisoned by king Drust.

entry U728.4
The battle of Monidhcrobh between the Picts themselves, in which Aengus was victor, and many were slain on the side of king Eilpín. A woeful battle was fought between the same parties near Caissel Créidi, where Eilpín was put to flight.

entry 729.2
The battle of Monid Carno near Loch Laegde between the hosts of Nectan and the army of Aengus, and Nectan's exactors fell i.e. Biceot son of Monet, and his son, Finnguine son of Drostan, Feroth son of Finnguine, and many others; and the adherents of Aengus were triumphant.

entry U729.3
The battle of Druim Derg Blathug in the territory of the Picts between Aengus and Drust, king of the Picts, and Drust fell.

[CELT URL]

It has been suggested the first battle here took place at Moncrieff Hill between the Tay and Earn rivers just south-east of Perth. Smyth makes much of the term *Exactores* used by Bede in his description of the battle of Monith Carno between Angus and Nechtan in 729CE, suggesting it to mean tax-collectors. If true this would suggest that the institution of kingship was well entrenched by the period as the gathering in of taxes is a clear example of a centralised state. However Woolf has shown [2006a, p.132] that this is a misreading and that the reference in the *Annals of Ulster* should simply be read as Angus defeating his enemies in general. This matters because although we seem to be in a situation where apparently there is a widespread dynastic struggle taking place, we have no evidence to tell us that the basic tribal structure of Pictish society has been substantively altered. Tax-collectors would suggest that significant changes had happened in the structure of such a society. I would suggest that at this period the kings referred to, whatever their actual precise societal position, would be very unlikely to be raising taxes. It is much more likely that they would rely on the traditional pattern of peripatetic kingship in which the king, high-chief or leader of a tribal society would live in turn amongst different groups, each of which would be expected to keep him and his retinue for a specified period. This was common amongst tribal peoples throughout Eurasia and still exists to some extent amongst tribal peoples in other parts of the world. It was a standard practice amongst tribal peoples, including the Highland clans, for the chief to hold stocks of food, gathered from amongst the tribe, against times of need and to support those who could not support themselves and this type of surplus could well be used to provide the feeding of a peripatetic high-chief or king and his retinue.

Describing the Highlands pre-1745 Keltie tells us:

> The land was regarded not so much as belonging absolutely to the chief, but as the property of the clan of which the chief was head and representative. Not only was the clan bound to render obedience and reverence to their head, to whom each member supposed himself related, and whose name was the common name of all his people; he also was regarded as bound to maintain and protect his people, and distribute among them a fair share of the lands which he held as their representative. The chief, even against the laws, is bound to protect his followers, as they are

sometimes called, be they never so criminal. He is their leader in clan quarrels, must free the necessitous from their arrears of rent, and maintain such who, by accidents, are fallen into decay. If, by increase of the tribe, any small farms are wanting, for the support of such addition he splits others into lesser portions, because *all must be somehow provided for;* and as the meanest among them pretend to be his relatives by consanguinity, they insist upon the privilege of taking him by the hand wherever they meet him.

[1830, p.391]

Tax-collecting which suggests some sort of money exaction is clearly different from this. We do not know how extensive the use of money was at this period, though coinage had been known since Roman times. As far as I am aware no one has as yet tried to define exactly how kingship arose in Scotland but it would seem obvious that in societies like those of the Picts and the Scots it would have had to develop directly from earlier tribal practices, rather than have been created by incomers.

The King Lists tell us that Nechtan managed to rule briefly for some part of 728CE but by 729 Angus was secure in his position. Smyth refers [*Ibid*, p.75] to 'a multiplicity of Pictish kings' and there are references in the Annals to kings of the Picts, of Scotland and of Fortriu. Without wishing to belabour the point, if we think of Pictish society as still being essentially tribal, each of these titles can be seen as more like area chieftains, rather than kings, in the sense of single rulers of a specific political entity. Such entities could be formed on the basis of a collection of different communities who were united by common descent or societal practice such as inter-marriage, or could possibly include all those within a specified geographical area. Given the potentially fluid nature of tribal society, these two conditions should not be thought of as mutually exclusive, and it is probable that there were variations in how high-chiefs functioned from area to area. The term *mormaor,* which survived into the 11th century and which has been interpreted as being effectively the ruler of a Pictish province, should perhaps be understood in this way. The only substantial settlements as yet excavated from the Pictish period are monasteries and we lack evidence to support the existence of a politically structured society requiring a permanent central capital. There is clear evidence of continuity of use on such hilltop sites as Traprain Law and elsewhere from the Iron Age, and possibly earlier, and such locales would appear to have been fulfilling the role of tribal capitals, rather than representing any greater degree of centralisation. We should also remember that such hilltop sites had a range of tribal functions, partly sacral, partly social and were never simply military establishments.

It is unclear whether the combatants in the struggles of the 720s were leading separate tribes or larger groupings composed of warriors from different tribes, but the references suggest a condensed period of pronounced military activity which itself suggests a struggle for control in which Angus proved triumphant. It is therefore perhaps of some significance that the report of the *Annals of Ulster* 729.2 states that it was the 'adherents of Aengus' that were triumphant, rather than 'Aengus' himself. In a tribal context these adherents would be members of his kin-group and most probably those closest to him and thus to their common ancestor, suggesting that they would be that section of the tribe from whom rulers were traditionally chosen. That is not to say they were an aristocracy, even if their status among their own kin was greater than any other section of that extended kin-group. From the point of view of a distant scribe the niceties of power structures within such tribes would be an irrelevance.

Angus' battles are obviously of great significance in that he remained as king for another three decades, though sadly the battle sites, like many places referred to in the early Annals from Ireland or England, are difficult, if not impossible, to locate. The battle in which Angus defeated Alpin, in 728CE, is referred to in the *Annals of Tigernach as* taking place at 'Moin-craibe' [Anderson 1992, p.223] and, as noted, it has been suggested that this may well have been Moncrieff Hill. Further north in Perthshire there is a local tradition of Angus having fought Drest on the slopes of Blath Bhalg above Strathardle and a few miles north-west of Kirkmichael. The name in the original Annals is '*Druim Derg Blathug*', the first two parts of which mean red ridge, an understandable name for a battle site. The story in Strathardle is quite specific and says that after the battle there were so many slain that there were too many for the survivors to bury and the bodies were dumped in Lochan Dubh on the southeast shoulder of the hill. Given the lack of early Scottish historical sources might it not be worth emulating the procedure of Schliemann who located Troy by following the 'story' of Homer's *Iliad* and investigating the lochan? The location and excavation of a Pictish battle site might help settle a particular question. While we know that the indigenous tribes appear to have had the capacity to rally in large numbers as Tacitus claims happened at Mons Graupius and as surely must have happened at Dunnichen and some of the other battles against the invading Angles from Northumbria, we cannot be so certain of the numbers involved in battles such as took place in the 720s. If these were the working out of a dynastic struggle or an attempt by one, or a group of tribes, to become dominant, those involved in the battle may well have been little more than a war-band. As already stated such war-bands would have been modelled on the groups organised for inter-tribal raiding and would have numbered in the tens rather than hundreds. In the late Highland period such raiding bands often numbered a dozen or less. We are perhaps misled by the constant reference to kings into thinking of the massed armies of later times.

The focus of recent Pictish archaeology has been on religious sites and while these can advance our knowledge of certain aspects of contemporary life they cannot answer basic questions regarding the structure of day-to-day Pictish society. Even in a society where all men were expected to have military skills we cannot be sure whether the battles referred to in the Annals were large-scale military actions or, in modern terms, little more than skirmishes. If, as the result of such a skirmish, a person considered important died, it would in all likelihood be recorded. The act of recording it does not tell us the numbers involved. It should be noted that the struggles in Dalriada around this period between the different tribes there might also be better understood as likewise involving war-bands rather than armies. Without clear evidence it is impossible to be sure either way.

Whatever the actual numbers involved it is clear that by 731CE Angus had apparently become dominant within Pictish society. In that year his son Talorc was involved in a battle, at a place the *Annals of Tigernach* refers to as Muirbolg, with Scots from Dalriada under Brude, the son of Congus. Here we have the name Brude referring to a Scot from the West, showing that a name occurring several times in the Pictish King Lists was used among the Q-Celtic speaking Scots of the west and suggesting perhaps that the linguistic differences between the two societies may not have been as significant as modern scholarship tends to suggest. Of course given the possibility of the Pictish kings coming from without strictly Pictish society, perhaps the name is not itself Pictish. However there are other instances of names occurring both within Pictland and Dalriada and this suggests that trying to understand these divergent societies as being substantially differentiated by language may not be particularly helpful. There is clear evidence of inter-marriage at a 'royal' level, and given the nature of the small-scale settlement of contemporary Scotland, a situation that carried on throughout most of the country till at least the 17th century, it is likely there would have been very close contact where the two societies overlapped. At the conference founding the Elphinstone Institute in Aberdeen, in 1996, Professor Sandy Fenton made a comment regarding later Scottish society, which is highly relevant to how we might better see our past. He said that the idea of the Highland Line while it is precise in geographical terms was not nearly so clear in terms of human interaction. Discussing linguistic patterns and social interaction he suggested that we would be better looking at the area as a 'Highland sausage', meaning that there was an area of mutual social and linguistic inter-penetration on either side of the geographical fault line. The modern idea of rigid, set borders between nations does not fit in First Millennium Scotland and the consequent notion of strict mono-lingualism within defined areas is no more likely to be a precise fit.

As both Picts and Scots were pastoral, warrior societies inhabiting the same environment and speaking variants of what is generally accepted as a once common source language, they would have had much in common with each other, and possibly little other than language that set them apart. We cannot be sure that either the Picts or Scots defined themselves by their languages, their loyalty to the tribe ensuring that their view of the world was defined by the relationship to their kin, and their ancestors, rather than any external concept of nationhood, however defined. Modern ideas of ethnicity, defined in such essentially linguistic terms as 'Anglo-Saxon', 'Celtic' or 'Germanic' would have had no relevance to the people living in Scotland in the First Millennium. Although the tribe is defined by people living in kin-groups claiming descent from a common ances-tor, there must have been some social fluidity. It is at least possible that groups who inter-married did not always share their first language. Professor Fenton's concept of the 'Highland sausage' may well have had more localised variants and it is a fact that humans in many societies throughout the world are often bi- or even tri-lingual. Nowadays, living in nation states, we think of ourselves as members of the community of such political entities, the Pictish tribes did not. Scots living in small kin-groups near Pictish settlements, occupied by people with whom they had much in common, would likely be similar. Our modern ideas of nationality and statehood are precise in ways which would have not been understood by the people of First Millennium Scotland and we must be constantly aware of problems arising from imposing our own ideas on distant societies on the basis of linguistic analysis which is itself a product of the modern world.

That the two societies were still in close contact in the eighth century is underlined by a singular Annal reference for 734CE, again from the *Annals of Tigernach*. It says that Talorc, son of Congus, who had defeated Angus' son Brude at Muirbolg, handed his own brother over to the Picts who proceeded to 'bind' him, then drown him. Apart from the fact that again we seem to have the same names in both groups this suggests a level of co-operation at a leadership level, even if in this situation it is rather gruesome. Given what has been said above, contacts at this level are likely to have been echoed by others at a more localised level. The existence of a Pictish style boar, carved into the living rock on the top of Dunadd, probably the most important site for the Dalriadan Scots, is perhaps an instance of common cultural ideas rather than evidence of conquest or dynastic shift. In the same year Talorcan, son of Drostan, who is elsewhere referred to as king of Athole, was captured near Dunolly, near Oban and imprisoned. It does not say by whom he was imprisoned but it would seem that he was on some form of raid into Argyll when he was captured. Angus then appears to have attacked Dalriada, forcing the then king Dungal, son of Selbach, to flee to Ireland. Two years later Angus is back ravaging Dalriada, taking the capital of Dunadd and capturing Dungal and his brother Feradach. Angus' son Brude died soon after. Angus' brother Talorcan then led the Picts in battle against Ainfcellach's son Muiredach in Argyll and forced him to flee. The reference to this in the *Annals of Ulster* says that 'many nobles died'. These reports suggest that in this period the Picts were dominant over the Scots. As we have no clear knowledge of exactly how the tribal societies of the Picts and Scots functioned, this reference to 'nobles' must be treated with caution. There is no reason to assume that this refers to some sort of structured hierarchy akin to that of later feudalism, and the status of those to whom 'nobles' refers is, within a society where the function of the warrior was absolutely central, as likely to have been to do with martial prowess as birth. In the midst of this there is a reference to the death of Owen, king of the Picts which Anderson notes [1990, p.325] is likely to be a mistaken entry for Ewan, or Eogan who was actually a king of the Scots and a brother of Selbach and Ainfcellach.

In 739CE it is said that Angus drowned Talorcan, son of Drostan who was king of Athole. This can be seen as Angus further consolidating his power and in 741CE he is back fighting the Dalriadans and seems to have effectively conquered them. The focus then shifts and the Annals tell us that the Picts and Britons of Strathclyde were at war by 744CE. However the fortunes of battle turned against Angus and in 750CE he lost his brother Talorcan and another unnamed brother in a battle against the Britons after which the Annals say his power was reduced. While Angus held on to the throne there is a report of a further battle amongst the Picts in Circenn, probably referring to the east coast area north of Dundee, in which Brude, son of Maelchion died. This suggests that Brude may well have been the reason for Angus' decline in power through pressing his own claims to overall control amongst the Picts. Angus was to remain as king till his death in 761CE and thus seems to have success- fully seen off all challengers to his authority and there are no references in the Annals to any battles involving the Picts in the last 10 years of his life. The battles of the 720s and 730s do seem to have had dynastic over- tones and given the volatile nature of the times, and the essentially tribal structure of the societies involved it is possible that Angus felt it neces- sary to attack both the Scots of Dalriada and the Britons of Strathclyde to stabilise his own power, rather than attempting to extend Pictish authority over these neighbouring peoples.

Given the incursions by the Northumbrians and the frequent records of battle with their other southern neighbours it would appear that con- solidating the Pictish position would be a practical move, following the old adage that attack is the best form of defence. We should keep in mind however that even with the influence of the expanding Church and the stresses caused by Northumbrian expansion over the previous century, the Picts, Britons and Scots are still essentially not just tribal structures but warrior societies, and battle, rather than war, was an accepted, and expected, part of their existence. We must surely therefore veer to the side of caution when trying to attribute political motives which may be anachronistic. As I have already suggested we are in a period where the loose tribal structures of earlier times certainly seem to be changing but how fast and to what extent is, as yet, unclear.

A section of Bower's *Scotichronicon*, composed in the 1440s and thus in no way contemporaneous might serve to illustrate how closely the societies of Scots and Picts were entwined, and to what extent they were basically warrior societies. This story is worth repeating here in full:

In the time of this Diocletian (Roman Emperor 284–316) or a little before, while the nations of the Scots and Picts were living peacefully together in their two kingdoms, it happened by chance that on a prearranged day certain noblemen from both nations met together, as was their custom, on the borders of the kingdoms for some hunting. While the dogs were unleashed and they were running about in all directions chasing wild beasts for about the length of a day, a certain hound, which used to follow the scent on the tracks of the beasts, was stolen away by the Picts, and was immediately discovered in their possession. When the Scots demanded it back [the Picts] refused to return it. A dispute arose and the [Scots] tried to snatch it from them by force. But the Picts for their part made no attempt to mitigate their wrong-doing by giving them satisfaction, but rather made matters worse by even greater savagery, and they lost no time in starting to fight. As a result many on both sides of those who had met together were slain by each other's swords. For this was the occasion and beginning of the first dispute between them, as we read, after they had lived together in unbroken peace for five hundred years, and had joined harmoniously together in resisting all other nations with their united power. But soon after this, just as formerly their friendship with each other was keenly fostered by frequent exchange of kind services, by the alliances between their children, by the strong bonds of matrimony and also by frequent reciprocal dinner parties, as if they were one people, so with all the more savagery their enmity increased from day to day with plundering, arson, slaughter and ambushes, and various disturbances and eruptions. And although secure peace and terms of truce were frequently agreed between them, the situation deteriorated, so that the one people was exerting all its determination to destroy the other. Peace however was restored by Carausis the Briton, when he proposed to take them with him to fight against the Romans...

[Watt Vol 1, p.265]

While this can in no way be seen as accurate historical reporting, it is interesting that in the 15th century the component parts of the Scottish nation – Picts and Scots – were seen as having been so involved with each other. While Carausis was in fact a Roman general who unsuccessfully attempted to take over the Empire in 286CE from his power base in Britain, the picture of how a fight could break out between two groups of armed warriors makes sense and in fact is echoed by many later instances of bloodshed between clans during the Middle Ages.

The increasing number of references in the Annals to affairs amongst the Picts in the first half of the eighth century can be understood as a direct result of the volatile political situation and the years after Angus' death in 761CE are not covered to anything like the same extent. Strangely his death, recorded in the *Annals of Ulster* in 761CE, is preceded by an entry 10 years earlier that reads 'U750.11 End of the reign of Aengus'. Perhaps this is nothing more than an error but we cannot rule out the possibility that he had assumed the role of leader of the Picts at an earlier period and had then been deposed.

The decrease in the number of references to the Picts of course could simply mean that the information channels between the land of the Picts and Ireland had in some way been interrupted in this period but given the now established power of the Catholic Church in most, if not all, of the British Isles, this appears unlikely. It may simply be that a new abbot was in charge of the monastery where the original Annal was being created and he had little interest in affairs outside of Ireland.

In 763CE Brude, given as king of Fortriu, who appears to be Angus' successor, died, and five years later a battle is said to have taken place in Fortriu between Aed and Kenneth. Kenneth, given as Cinoid in some versions of the list, was the successor of Brude and Aed was the king of Dalriada, so if Fortriu is, as Woolf suggests, in the north, then Aed must have been leading a raid to the north. Both men survived the battle and given the lack of available sources for the period we have no information to help us unravel what the political reasons, or effects, of this battle were. In 775CE Kenneth died to be succeeded by Alpin, son of Wroid. In 778CE we have a unique reference to the Picts. The *Annals of Ulster* tell us that Ethne, daughter of Kenneth, died. This is the first and last time that a Pictish woman is mentioned directly in the Annals – references to any women are rare – and while this lack is hardly surprising given the attitude of the Christian Church towards women as the root of all sin, why is Ethne mentioned? She is not said to have been of particular note as a holy person but her appearance may be linked to the possibility already mentioned that the King Lists contain the names of mothers as well as fathers of kings. If the Picts were matrilineal it would certainly not be something to which the Church would like to draw attention. As usual the lack of indigenous records ensures that it is impossible to ascertain who this Ethne was, other than the daughter of a king, which according to the model presented above would mean that she herself would not be a part of the line of sovereignty. Perhaps she had come to the attention of the scribes who compiled the Annals, as a leader of a nunnery, or through being known for being particularly devout. Elsewhere I have noted [McHardy 2003, 2005] that the role of women in the pre-Christian religion was apparently extensive and this combined with the possibility of ongoing matrilineal succession may well have meant that women continued to have a significant role in Pictish society despite the dominance of the Catholic Church. It is noticeable that Forbes, *Kalendar of Scottish Saints*, which is a collection of traditions relating to supposed early Christian activists in Scotland, contains a considerable number of females, some of whom I have noted are based on clear pre-Christian models [McHardy 2003].

In 780CE Alpin son of Wroid died and was succeeded by Drest, son of Talorcan. In the *Annals of Ulster* for that year is the statement that 'Alpin, king of the Saxons, died.' Anderson [1992, p.243] suggests that this should be read as meaning that there were Saxons within the lands under Alpin's control. He further suggests that the origin of his name may well have been Aelfwine, an Anglian name he suggests may have come about through his mother being English. He further suggests that the text may have been corrupted but the title King of the Saxons is certainly strange, unless of course it means, as Anderson puts forward [*Ibid*, p.253] that Alpin had control of the Lothians. Even if the Northumbrian expansion into the Lothians had resulted in extensive settlement there is no reason to assume that the original native people were either wiped out or forced to move elsewhere. Such activity would surely have found some mention in the Annals. The original P-Celtic speaking tribes of the Gododdin may have faded from history but their descendants must have continued to live in the Lothians and this may well have had something to do with possible Pictish control of the area. During the ongoing struggle for control of the Lothians, the inhabitants, particularly if still essentially tribal, may well have done what tribespeople often do, and switched allegiance between powerful entities to ensure maximum benefit for themselves. This type of behaviour can be seen in the Middle Ages when Lords of the Isles were quite capable of entering into alliances with kings of England against the kings of Scots, to whom they felt no particular loyalty.

However as has already been noted there are place names throughout the lands of the Picts that refer variously to other people and if these were indeed settlements of foreigners the idea that there were Saxons amongst them is anything but impossible. The matter of course is complicated by the modern understanding of these terms which places great stress on the language such groups supposedly spoke. We cannot know if the Picts saw the Saxons as a specific people or just another set of foreign warriors.

In 782CE there is a mention of the death of Dubthalorc in the *Annals of Ulster* and he is said to be 'king of the Picts this side of the Mounth'. This is the first time such a description is used, and has generally been taken to mean that he was a sub-king under Drest. Throughout the period from the sixth to the ninth centuries there are differing references to various rulers or leaders as either kings of the Picts or of Fortriu in the main Annal sources, those of Ulster and of Tigernach. It is noticeable that these different terminologies never appear together. We either hear of a king of Fortriu or of a king of the Picts, rarely even Pictland. Are we seeing a reflection of a truly dual kingdom as has been suggested on many occasions, or are we seeing what are merely alternative descriptive terms for what is essentially the same position? This last possibility could have occurred if there were different original Scottish Annal sources being accessed by the scribes compiling the surviving Annals in Ireland. While this is not supportive of my contention that the Picts were essentially a congregation of different tribes for most of their history, it does serve to make clear the fact that we are dealing with historical sources that not only survive through much later copies, but that those original sources were compiled outside of the land of the Picts by people who are very unlikely to have had any personal contact with, or knowledge of Pictish society.

Alex Woolf has suggested [2006 *passim*] that Fortriu was likely to have been the area now known as Moray in the north. If this is the case then Fortriu certainly had some strategic advantages. The problems with the neighbouring polities of Northumbria, Dalriada and Strathclyde all brought various stresses to bear on the Picts but if their capital, or political centre, was on the other side of the Grampian mountains from these troublesome neighbours, it would be much less susceptible to being over-run at any time from the south. This might also mean that the necessary retrenchment that appears to have taken before the victory at Dunnichen would have taken place beyond the ken of the Northumbrians. Most commentators on the Picts have been happy to accept that Fortriu was those lands we now know as Strathearn and Menteith though Broun [2005, p.38] suggests that it may well have lain more to the north-east and run as far as Dunnottar, near Stonehaven. This problem is compounded by the fact that great reliance has been placed on one particular document to try to understand the layout and political structure of Pictland. This is the document known as *De Situ Albanie*, compiled no earlier than the early years of the 13th century. In her ground-breaking book *The Picts*, Isobel Henderson made the point that this '...is a much more careless piece of work than writers have admitted and its evidence should not be given too much weight.' [1967, p.36]. It is this document that presents Pictland as being divided into seven different provinces, each of which is a combination of two contiguous areas. These provinces are closely related to the origin myth in Gaelic which mentions seven sons of the eponymous ancestor Cruithne, the usual name for the Picts in early Gaelic sources. More recently Dauvit Broun [2005] has analysed this material, making the point that although this is essentially a scholarly attempt to try and present a cohesive picture of what Pictland would have been like, it is one that cannot be said with any authority to conform to what reality was on the ground.

Woolf [2006, p.201] refers back to the Roman writer Ammianus who said the peoples of northern Britain were divided into two peoples, the Dicalydones and the Verturiones. He says that as the Caledonians seem to have been present in the Central Highlands, quoting Ptolemy's map and the place names Dunkeld and Rohallion as evidence, then the Verturiones should be seen as being north of this. As has been pointed out the differentiation between two separate Pictish groups first mentioned by Dio, clearly refers to the whole of modern Scotland and not just the area north of the Forth–Clyde line. However Woolf quotes further evidence including the 13th century *Prophecy of Berchan*, containing a section on the Kings of Ireland and Scotland, which says that in the late 10th century King Dub was killed in '*Mag Fortren*', the Plain of Fortriu which is explicitly said to be beyond the Mounth, the outlying spur of the Grampians that approaches the sea near Stonehaven [2006, p.196]. He also quotes another source that Dub was killed at Forres and buried at Kinloss [*Ibid*] and other sources that suggest Fortriu was in fact in the north.

The likelihood may well be that the terms Fortriu and the land of the Picts were effectively interchangeable and that any political division between north and south Pictland must remain unclear. What is clear is that although there are ongoing battles between the Picts and the Scots in the latter half of the eighth century the disruption surrounding the eventual victory of Angus in the 720s had passed and there may well have been a more peaceful period towards the end of the century. The specific description of Dubthalorc as king 'south of the Mounth' suggests that even if Angus and his successors were based in the north, kingly power, such as it was, was now located in the south.

In 780CE Alpin was succeeded by Drest, son of Talorcan and there seems to have been a further period of internal unrest. According to the *Chronicle of the Picts*, one of the lists of kings published by WF Skene in 1867, Drest ruled for one year only to be succeeded by Talorcan, son of Drostan, who four or five years later was followed by another Talorcan, son of Angus. The *Annals of Ulster* refer as noted above to Dubthalorc dying in 782CE. The first part of this name is clearly *dubh*, Gaelic for dark, giving us Talorc the Dark and Talorcan is a diminutive form of that name. Anderson suggests [1992, p.253] that this was Talorc, Angus' son, and notes that Skene thought this was Angus who had been king until 761CE. If so this would be an unusual instance of a son following his father to the position of king of the Picts. However we should also take note that the names Drest and Drostan are similar and as the various surviving texts of the Annals and King Lists show great variety in the spelling of personal names perhaps what we are seeing here is simply confusion on the part of the scribes copying ancient vellum texts in the early Middle Ages. If so it is possible that Talorcan son of Drostan was the son of Drest, another instance of son following father. Anderson suggests that this Talorcan was a sub-king but as we have seen, the identity of the separate provinces of the Picts is dubious and we are never directly told of kings of the Picts and of Fortriu co-existing. The confusion that arises from our lack of corroboration might be best dealt with by accepting some scribal error in this period. In 789CE there is reference in the *Annals of Ulster* to Conall, Tadc's son being defeated by Constantine in a 'battle among the Picts'. Conall is also mentioned in the *Pictish Chronicle* so would have followed on from Talorcan, and this is noted in other versions of the King List as happening in 784CE. The simplest reading is that Talorcan, whoever his father or mother was, followed Drest and was replaced by Conall in 784CE. With Constantine we are on surer ground. He was king for a long time but it was to be a time of great stress as once again the Picts were forced to fight invaders.

The eighth century had opened with a period of consolidation following successful resistance to attempted conquest from the south and was to close with a series of raids from the north that came close to overthrowing Constantine's kingship and the very independence of the Pictish people.

CHAPTER TEN

The end of the Picts?

AS THE EIGHTH CENTURY drew to a close a new force was about to enter into the lives of the Pictish peoples. The close relationship with Dalriada, in which several kings appear to have ruled over both areas simultaneously, has been interpreted in several ways. It has often been said to denote the beginning of a Gaelic takeover of the Picts. This is nonsensical as Gaelic is a language and the idea of a separate ethnicity between the Scots and Picts has been exploded by the recent work of Brian Sykes on the genetic make-up of Britain. He said, 'The maternal gene pool is more or less the same in Pictland, in "Celtic" Argyll and in the Highlands' [2006, p.209]. He further notes that there are strong similarities in the male gene pool between Argyll and Ireland. Given the close and ongoing contact between these areas over the past few millennia that is hardly surprising. Another way of looking at this has been as a dynastic takeover of Pictland by Gaelic-speaking Scots. As we have seen, the Picts had long been in the habit of having men elsewhere assume the role of king. Dauvit Broun [Foster 1998, pp.71–84] has suggested that in this period what we see is in fact a true dynasty, in the sense of succession through an identifiable, in this case essentially masculine, direct blood line starting with Onuist son of Urguist who died in 761. Allowing for the extreme scarcity of surviving contemporary evidence he has put forward the following family tree, suggesting that it is Pictish.

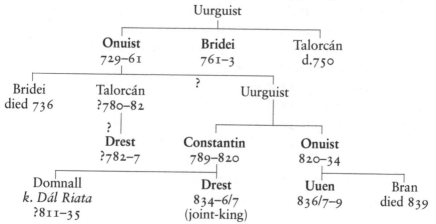

This makes sense and would perhaps go some way to explaining how the Picts managed to see off the Vikings. The ability to lead effective resistance against ongoing raids which at times must have appeared little different from large-scale invasion, would require someone to act not just as military strategist but as a long term leader who could provide the focus for logistical and tactical planning.

The Vikings were much more successful than any earlier invaders, settling in the north and much of the west of the country, and considerable areas of Scotland remained under Norse control into the Middle Ages. This success and the regularity of raids from the north could not but serve to further consolidate Pictish power structures. Even if the basic constituent of Pictish society was still the scattered kin-groups of their ancestors, they would need some way of uniting in times of such danger much more often than in the past. By the dawn of the ninth century we can posit that 'kingship' among the Picts would have taken on more than the temporary needs of specific military campaigns. Although we may never know how the Picts themselves saw their kings, and as noted most interpretations to date have been overly influenced by later, essentially feudal models with complex and hierarchical court structures – for which there is no evidence – we must surely accept that by that time the Vikings were attacking, Constantine would have had the capacity to, at the least, raise troops across all the lands of the Picts. Given what we know of later Scottish Highland society, even this would require a widespread acceptance of the king's role by a disparate set of groups, each united by loyalty to its own defined kin-group. We cannot even be sure that the Pictish tribes were, like that later Highland society, essentially agnatic, i.e. inheritance, rights, obligations and status came through the male line. However if Broun's family tree of the descendants of Urguist is correct then we can clearly see that there is a move towards this sort of structure, even if only at the top end of Pictish society.

Constantine is said in the *Annals of Ulster* to have come to the kingship of the Picts/Fortriu by defeating Conall, Tadc's son in 789CE [Anderson 1990, p.254]. This Conall was later killed by another Conall, son of Aedan, in 807CE who replaced him as king of Dalraida. A few years later in 811CE, the King Lists for Argyll tell us that Constantine had become king of the Scots of Dalriada, a position he held till his death. Clearly the interpenetration of Pictish and Scottish society was considerable and I would suggest we have been led into a misunderstanding of both societies by seeing this interpenetration as happening only at the dynastic level. If they were sharing a supreme leader and fighting against a common enemy over any extended period, this would have led to increased contact between the two different peoples at many levels of society, even if such contact had not previously been the norm. This concentration on dynastic level activity combined with the over-emphasis on the suggested differences in language, with the implication of the Picts as monoglot P-Celtic speakers and the Scots as monoglot Q-Celtic speakers has created a tendency to perceive of both groups forming something like modern nation states. This is highly dubious, precisely because the inherent tribalism of both groups, better attested in Dalriadan sources, whether or not contemporaneous with a kingship structure, would work against the creation of anything like a modern nation state. The later examples of the Highlands, the Borders and Dumfries and Galloway already mentioned, illustrate the difficulties inherent in trying to control all of Scotland from a single centre, something that can be persuasively argued did not come about till nearly a thousand years after Constantine's time.

Barbara Crawford makes a telling point about the Viking incursions from the north when she writes

> ... the fact that all the peoples of Scandinavia – Danes, Swedes and Norwegians – were involved in this movement does suggest that there must have been some common features in the nature of their economic or social development or in the stage of their relationship with western Europe which were responsible for this phenomenon. There is a long-standing explanation of over-population and land-shortage in Scandinavia... [which] ... does suggest that the nature of the home environment may have played a part in stimulating their movement, first of all the northern peoples because agricultural resources were more limited in Norway than in Denmark.

[1987, p.42]

A further factor in the original surge of raiding was the development of longship technology. The sailing skills of the Vikings are justly renowned and the eventual influence the Norsemen came to have over most of the British Isles in the ensuing centuries is testament to their military skills and seamanship. That the Vikings were avid traders as well as brutal raiders is well attested and the likelihood is that some of those who came on the early raids had been to Britain before. As Crawford says,

> In the trading pattern of north Europe, the natural products of the northern lands – furs, walrus-ivory and ropes, amber from the Baltic – were all highly-valued commodities.
>
> [*Ibid*, p.43]

In the case of amber the trading had been going on since prehistoric times, with gold going in the other direction. The outstanding skills of the Norsemen were built on millennia of water-borne transport and as we have seen, there is a great deal of archaeological evidence showing that contact between northern Britain and Scandinavia and the Low Countries was already long established by this period. As Cunliffe has shown [2001, pp.484ff], trading activity and contact around the North Sea was a well established fact by this period, and this had led to the development of wealthy trading centres, which like the growing Christian monasteries were a tempting target for the pagan raiders from the North.

The first mention of these raids in the *Annals of Ulster* tells us that all of the British Isles were suddenly subjected to raiding. In fact all the surviving Annals from the period are full of detail about the devastating attacks from the north for decades. Most of the surviving records refer to raids on the west coast of Scotland, very little has survived about the east coast raids, other than in folklore and in the stories of various martyred saints. However the extent of material, often linking 'Danish' attacks to First Millennium, or older, ancient monuments is testament to the fact that here too the Vikings had a significant effect.

There are many references in the Annals to attacks on monasteries but also reports of widespread cattle lifting and whole islands being laid waste by the invaders. The monasteries with their rich altar-ware of gold and silver and their holdings of food and raw materials were a natural target for the raiders. It is fair to say that monasteries such as those on Iona and elsewhere were the First Millennium equivalent of towns, the rest of the population still living in small communities scattered around the landscape. The Vikings at this stage had not been Christianised, many areas of Scandinavia remaining pagan into the Second Millennium, and there was thus no restraint in their dealing with monks and priests. From the point of view of the northern raiders the priests were fair game and it is clear from contemporary reports that many of these raids were extremely brutal. Surviving Annals from both Ireland and England tell of repeated raids year on year. The raids continued for much of the century and in time were accompanied by the Vikings settling. While many of the raids were carried out by handfuls of longships with up to a couple of hundred raiders, there were also some years when the Northmen arrived in much greater force. They were successful in taking over most of Scotland north of Inverness, the Hebrides and the northern isles of Orkney and Shetland, and they came close to totally conquering the Picts on at least one occasion.

A flavour of the times can be caught in the story of the martyrdom of Blathmac son of Fland, on Iona in 825CE. His death is mentioned in the *Annals of Ulster* and a later *Life of Blathmac* gives greater detail. It tells us that he went to Iona with a group of other monks well aware of what their fate was likely to be. Blathmac is portrayed as courageously refusing to tell a group of invading Vikings where there was gold on the island, and 'being torn limb from limb' as a result [Anderson 1990, p.265]. Like a lot of material arising from within the Church the clear purpose of this story is essentially propagandistic. If Blathmac had gone to his death snivelling and crying for mercy, there is no chance we would hear of that. Such martyrdom was however not unique. As late as the 870s Adrian and his followers are said to have been massacred on the Isle of May, in the Firth of Forth, by yet another band of ravening Vikings. Like many early Christian sites the Isle of May seems to have previously been a site of some sacred significance, a fact which underlines the continuity of culture from prehistoric into Pictish times. What is striking about Blathmac is that he is presented as deliberately going out to seek martyrdom – the red martyrdom of death, shedding one's blood for Christ as opposed to the white martyrdom in which the devotee willingly gives up worldly concerns and makes his or her life a perpetual pilgrimage. Blathmac's actions, ironically perhaps, would seem to have involved the sin of pride.

Whatever the precise relationship between the Iona foundation and other communities in Ireland, the communication between them was disrupted by the arrival of the Viking raiders and was to have an effect on Christianity in Pictland. Up to this period the role of Iona was, according to the records we have, which of course were created by monks under its influence, considerable, but being raided by Vikings three times in little over a decade meant it could no longer function as it had.

In 789 Constantine – referred to as Castantin – had defeated Conall son of Tadg in battle and taken over as king. During his long reign he not only managed to keep the Vikings from overrunning the whole of Scotland but appears to have been instrumental in the further development of the Christian Church. By 806CE Iona, although it was never completely abandoned by monks, could no longer exert great influence, which had partly arisen from its role in the time of Columba and partly from the manipulation of Columba's 'image' as an important native saint by the Catholic Church after the Synod of Whitby. This saw it develop as a powerful ecclesiastical power centre within the Church as a whole, known as the *familia Iae*, but it could not hope to continue in its pre-eminent position while subject to ongoing sea-raids. While many of its notable treasures – such as the illustrated manuscript now known as the *Book of Kells* which appears to have begun under the influence of Pictish Art on Iona itself – were moved to Ireland, Constantine made sure that a new power centre of Christianity was created within the land at Dunkeld of the Picts.

Whatever the situation on the ground, we can be sure that Constantine managed to fend off the Vikings from much of the heartland of the Picts. We do not know how much control was exercised over Orkney, Shetland, the Hebrides or even Caithness but all of these areas fell under Viking control over the ensuing years. If the Pictish kings had been in supreme control over all of these areas, and we cannot be certain about that, the incursions of the Vikings must have been seen as a great defeat. The year before Constantine's death there is an entry in the *Annals of Ulster* referring to Aed, son of Niall, king of Tara, being 'upon a campaign in Scotland' [Anderson 1990, p.261]. Tara was the ancient capital of Ireland and the title king of Tara may well mean king of Ireland here. It is unclear whether he was fighting the Picts or the Vikings. If the former he may well have been supporting some sort of Dalriadan political move against the Picts but alternatively he could have been offering help to the Scots, or even the Picts, against incoming raiders. If as I contend, we should perhaps interpret these references to kings being to men more akin to high-chiefs of a tribe, or confederation of tribes, then his campaign in Scotland may well have been brought about by some sort of familial commitment, as it seems likely that the tribal basis of Irish society was little different from that of the Picts. It is important to understand that this could have applied to a relationship with Picts as well as, or instead of the Scots, due to the mutual interpenetration already suggested.

Constantine continued as dual-king until his death in 820CE and according to version D of the Pictish King List [Anderson 1973, p.2766] he founded the religious centre at Dunkeld. This was perhaps in response to the Viking raids on Iona which made its continuance – as effectively the mother church of Pictland – untenable. While some of Iona's treasures went to Kells in Ireland others were taken to Dunkeld where the new foundation was set up. In a time of widespread raiding Dunkeld offered a greater degree of safety than other foundations of roughly the same period like St Andrews and Portmahomack in Easter Ross which, with their seaside locations, were all too open to assault from sea-borne raiders. Dunkeld, the name itself deriving from the earlier tribe of the Caledonii [Watson 1993, p.21], is set deep in the Highlands and the importance of continuity with the traditions of his Pictish ancestors may well have had a role in Constantine's selection of the locale. While we cannot be sure of just how personally involved he was, the relocation of what was really the mother church of Pictland was clearly a significant event and perhaps can be seen as an opportunity taken to decrease the influence of the Scots on matters Pictish. It is notable that on his death Constantine was not referred to as king of Dalriada but king of Fortriu and Anderson makes the point that apparently the annalists in Ireland in 820 and 834CE thought it 'more important that a man was king of Fortriu than that he was king of Dalriada' [*Ibid*, p.194]. No matter what later commentators may think this is clear contemporary support for the idea that Pictland was not seen as some sort of subsidiary of Dalraida and suggests that the continuing importance given to the influence from the west of Scotland, initially developed through the early Columban Church, is perhaps still being over-rated. The second date in the quote refers to the death of Constantine's brother Angus who followed him to the kingship in 820.

Just as his brother is said to have founded Dunkeld, Angus is credited with the foundation of St Andrews though we must always remember that the sources we have, in this case Pictish King List D, survive only in later copies. Angus ruled for 14 years after Constantine's death in 820CE and throughout this period the Annals are full of reports of incursions by the Vikings, including instances of wholesale capture of females and many churches being plundered. Interestingly there are a couple of references to Iona in this period:

> entry U829.3
> Diarmait, abbot of Í, went to Scotland with the halidoms of Colum Cille.

> entry U831.1
> Diarmait came *back* to Ireland with the halidoms of Colum Cille.
>
> [CELT, URL]

This reads like an attempt to reinstate the primacy of Iona by returning the relics of the great Columba but its short-lived provenance is testament to the ongoing raids and thus the fragility of such hopes. Like Constantine Angus also ruled Dalriada and we can be relatively certain that he was kept busy with raids on both the east and west coasts. While there is no direct historical evidence for incursions on the east, the story of Adrian, said to have been martyred on the Isle of May, and a tale associated with Camus' Cross at Panmure, near Dundee, associating it with the leader of a Danish raid, suggest that the east was just as open to attack as the west.

According to the legend of the founding of St Andrews, Angus was fighting in Argyll when the monk Regulus arrived in Fife with the relics of St Andrew. Angus' sons Eogannan, Nechtan and Finguine were said to have been with their mother Findchaem at Forteviot, a place of some significance, as we shall see. A version of how St Andrew became Scotland's patron saint which I have given elsewhere [McHardy 2006, p.153 ff], has Angus uniting with a king of Dalriada, said to have been his cousin Eochaidh, to repulse yet another Northumbrian assault from the south led by Athelstan. As he was himself king of Dalriada at the time this seems spurious, but reflects the reality that folklore traditions, unconcerned as they are with specific times and dates, and sometimes even personages, still reflect what people believed to have happened in the past. It is worth considering why St Andrew became the patron saint of Scotland rather than Columba. Was this an early political move on Angus' part stressing the importance of a locale in the east, St Andrews, over one in the west, Iona? If in this period there is an ongoing struggle for overall control of the dual kingdoms of the Picts and Scots, such a move would appear possible. However as the surviving sources are from so much later it is impossible to be definite. Angus on his death is referred to as king of Fortriu as was Constantine, and given Woolf's contention that Fortriu was in the north this is of some significance. If the power base of these brothers was in Morayshire their respective involvements, however tenuous, in the founding of major religious sites at Dunkeld and St Andrews so far away is surely a testament to their power and a clear indication that no matter how the majority of the Pictish peoples still lived, that the kingship was well established over all of the different tribes.

Angus died in 834CE to be succeeded by Drust, Constantine's son, who only ruled for a couple of years before being briefly succeeded by Talorcan, son of Uuthoil, in 837CE and then Drust's cousin Uuen, son of Angus, the same year. His reign only lasted a further two years, being followed by that of Uurad in 839CE, then Brude in 842CE, Kenneth in 843CE, Brude again in the same year, then Drust in 845CE who was succeeded by Kenneth MacAlpin in 848CE. After the long reigns of Constantine and Angus this is a remarkably quick series of reigns but we have little evidence to tell us why, other than the King Lists themselves. It is perhaps reflective of the ongoing problems with the Vikings. It is also in this period that mention is made in the Annals of someone who was to have major importance in the future development of Scotland. In 836CE Kenneth, son of Alpin, is said to have summoned help from Ireland to reinforce Dalriada, presumably against the Vikings [Anderson 1990, p.267]. Dalriada had of course been sharing a king with the Picts for some time, and at this point the King Lists of Argyll and the Picts both have Eoganan, son of Angus, as king [Anderson 1990, pp.cxii and xciii].

In 839CE a major battle is reported in the *Annals of Ulster*:

A battle was fought by the gentiles against the men of Fortriu, and in it fell Eoganan, Angus's son, and Bran Angus's son, and Aed, Boanta's son; and others too numerous to mention.

[*Ibid*, p.839]

Eoganan, otherwise Uuen, is yet another Pictish king to fall in battle and Aed is said in later texts to have been a king of Dalriada, possibly in conjunction with Eoganan's overall control. This underlines the vagueness of the term king. Not only does it disguise the fundamental reality of the tribal structure of contemporary society but we have many instances where there are said to be different kings at the same time. This could be due to lack of definitive information on the part of the scribes, or their masters, or alternatively to them trying to fit the realities of inter-tribal politics into a more structured world-view. It is thus a moot point whether the importance of kingly figures in the Christian created Annals was matched by their role within their own societies. The gentiles here are Norsemen, possibly Danes. The battle of 839CE had clearly had a potentially disastrous effect on the Picts and Scots and we can see the confusion of the years immediately after as reflecting a society in crisis. This certainly appears to have been a major battle and perhaps was a serious attempt at expanding Norse control over the whole of Scotland. If so, it failed.

With the advent of Kenneth, son of Alpin, the combined leadership of the two kingdoms was well on the way to becoming permanent. Sadly there are no directly contemporary records and the amalgamation of the kingdoms was for a long time interpreted as a conquest of the Picts by the Scots. Anderson makes the following point:

> By the 12th century it was evidently believed that Kenneth achieved his kingdom through the complete wiping-out of the Pictish nobility, by force or fraud. A story that this was done by a single act of treachery on the part of the Scots seems to have been current towards the end of the 11th century.
>
> [1973, p.196]

There are several reasons for doubting this could have happened. The idea of a population subjecting themselves to an incoming king because he had wiped out an indigenous aristocracy is anachronistic. As far as we can be sure, despite the growing power and centralising tendencies of the kingship, Scotland was still occupied by people who were living as they had always done, in small and relatively scattered groups across the countryside. While the advent of Christianity had undoubtedly forced considerable societal change there are no obvious grounds for believing that the populace was not still basically bound by the ties of kinship, or that the essentially warrior-based structure of the tribes had changed. Later in Scotland this type of kinship structure was essentially agnatic i.e. relying on male descent, as it developed in the clan system of the Highlands. However it is interesting to note that Phillpotts discerned kindred groups still having considerable power throughout northern Europe, including England till late in the Middle Ages [1910 *passim*].

Some of these were agnatic and cognatic simultaneously, i.e. claiming relationships through both male and female lines. Given the possibility of some sort of matrilineal system amongst the Picts, the tribes of this period may well have retained some of this tradition. The idea that the Picts were some sort of servile population ready to be bossed around by a small, aristocratic group of so-called nobles from the west, contradicts what we do know about the Picts. If, as we have seen, the Highland clans retained an armed warrior section of their number till the 18th century, why should we think of the ninth century Picts as being any less militarily capable? The constant references to battle throughout the previous centuries, compared to the specific reports of the Romans, and evidence such as the earlier epic poem *The Gododdin*, all point to this whole period being one where the adult males of the various kin-groups were still warriors. In such a case the removal of one level of leadership would simply result in the arising of a new series of leaders – from within the kin-group.

There is in fact no contemporary evidence to support a Scottish take-over of the Picts in the 840s. Constantine and Angus had already apparently ruled both areas earlier in the century and Kenneth is mentioned in the *Annals of Ulster*, the nearest we have to a true contemporary record:

858 Kenneth. Alpin's son. king of the Picts... died.

[Anderson 1990, p.287]

Here he is given as the king of the Picts, not of the Scots. The versions of his accession that have him variously swindling or slaughtering the Picts all survive only in medieval manuscripts, with no earlier provenance. Broun also makes the point that the unification of the two kingdoms at this precise point in time is hardly supported by the available contemporary sources. The idea of the military conquest of the Picts by Kenneth son of Alpin simply does not stand up. Broun tells us

The extreme weakness of the evidential basis for Cinaed's 'Scottish' takeover of Pictland is today widely recognised by scholars.

[2007, p.73]

He further makes the point that it is Kenneth's grandsons who are first said to be kings of Alba, a term that clearly refers to the combined lands of the Picts and the Scots, in the 10th century. Additionally Broun sees the term Alba, generally accepted as being a Gaelic term, as representing a continuity with the Pictish as well as the Scottish past. He tells us

> When the mother tongue of the Picts ceased to be Pictish and became Gaelic, Alba and Albannaig would naturally have been the words used for their country and for themselves, in exactly the same way that, in the thirteenth century many of their descendants, who no longer spoke Gaelic, referred to their country as 'Scotland' and to themselves as 'Scots' using the English (or Inglis) equivalent words for Alba and Albannaig.
>
> [*Ibid*, p.87]

I remain to be convinced that the whole of Scotland was ever Gaelic-speaking and would suggest that the language of the east coast and southern parts of Scotland in the 13th century, Scots, may well have been spoken for a considerable time before that. We do not know when P-Celtic – at one point apparently the tongue of the vast majority of the population of the northern half of the island – was last spoken, but it eventually died out in Scotland and while it may be fashionable in academic circles to blithely accept that Scots is a direct descendant of the Anglo-Friesian Germanic dialects, there are other possibilities. Jamieson in his *Dissertation on the Origin of the Scottish Language*, which he included as a preface to his ground-breaking *An Etymological Dictionary of the Scottish Language* [1879–82], puts forward the suggestion that the Picts spoke an early form of Scots. While in today's Celtic-besotted world this is an unpopular idea, it is not without merit. We should consider the probability that several languages were spoken amongst the Pictish peoples. After all we have ample proof of long-term ongoing cultural contact between the Gaels from the West and the Germanic-speaking raiders who made such an impact from 793CE onwards, following earlier trading contacts, and who ended up settling in large areas of Scotland as well as going on to play a seminal role in the development of the Gall-Gael Lordship of the Isles. There were obviously several languages being spoken within the earshot of the Picts and this may well have included a variety of Germanic dialects long before the great Viking invasions.

The *Annals of Ulster* continue to refer to the kingdom of the Picts after Kenneth's death. In 862 again the *Annals of Ulster* refer to the death of a Pictish king, this time Donald, Kenneth's brother. One of the later sources, *The Chronicle of the Kings of Scotland*, another medieval King List, tells us that during Donald's time 'the Gaels with their king made the rights and the laws of the kingdom (that are called) of Aed, Eochaid's son in Fortevoit' [Anderson 1990, p.291]. Exactly what this means is problematic. As the evidence suggests that the two communities continued to have some level of separate existence for quite a few years after this, the idea that it is a mark of Scottish (Dalriadan) domination appears unlikely. The location of Forteviot however is in itself suggestive. Much had been made of a supposed palace here, which, given the peripatetic nature of Scottish kingship well into the medieval period seems somewhat anachronistic, but the surviving Pictish carved door lintel from here, and the nearby magnificent Dupplin Cross (now in Dunning Church) suggests that it was a place of some considerable significance in the late Pictish period. The area surrounding Forteviot is rich in archaeological remains which include at least two probable henges showing that this was a considered a site of importance by the native peoples over millennia.

The *Annals of Ulster* go on to refer to Fortriu in 866CE and to the Picts in 871CE and in 904CE there is a reference to the men of Fortriu. The new name for what is now Scotland, Alba, had not yet come into common usage and it would appear that the total assimilation of the Picts, if such it was, could not have happened before this latest date.

What modern scholarship is beginning to recognise is that Alba, the forerunner of Scotland, was not definitely established before the dawn of the 10th century. This means that the Picts do not even begin to disappear from history until that time. Also whether or not they were being referred to as Picts, Albannaig or Scots would have been irrelevant to most of them anyway, if my contention that the tribal structure still held sway is correct. Modern histories are written from the point of view of national identities but this concept would itself have been anachronistic through most of the past. Certainly tribes did unite against common enemies but again, as Highland history clearly shows, people could unite in common cause with those with whom they were generally at odds.

Broun, commenting on the complications of trying to untangle Kenneth MacAlpin's actual ancestry through the fog of later politically driven interpretations tells us:

One way of making sense of all this would be to suppose that the kings of Alba were not, in reality, descended from Cenél nGabráin at all: the 'real' descendants of Gabrán were the progeny of Fergus Goll in Gowrie... Cinaed mac Ailpín's descendants, in reality, may simply have been in origin a Pictish royal lineage who had, at some point, been given the most royal Dál Riata ancestry that could be created from extant materials (such as a Dál Riata regal list).

[2008, p.24]

He also uses a term in this essay that is I believe of great significance. Referring to Anfcellach, said to have been a king of Dalriada at the close of the seventh century, he refers to him as 'head of the kindred', in this case the Cenél nGabráin, one of the four kindreds of Argyll. In terms of most of the Pictish period, if my contention as to the basic tribal structure of their society holds water, this might be a term that is more useful than 'king' or even 'chief'.

Kenneth MacAlpin died in 858CE to be succeeded by his brother Donald, and again the question must be asked – was this a succession based on the tribal concept of a chief's brother being the most suitable candidate for leadership because he was the closest surviving descendant of the common ancestor from whom the community as a whole claimed descent? Donald was himself to die four years later and it was during his reign that the declaration of the laws of the Gaels at Forteviot, referred to above, took place. Later chronicles state that both Kenneth and Donald were buried in Iona which appears to have been some sort of sacred site before Columba was given permission by the Picts to set up his church there. With this burial practice we are clearly seeing increasing royal type behaviour, though we must be aware of the possibility that later writers were attributing contemporary royal practice to the long dead sons of Alpin.

After Donald, whose short reign we can assume was subject to depredations by Vikings, probably including those now settled in Ireland, he was succeeded by his nephew, Kenneth's son Constantine. He reigned for 15 or 16 years and throughout this time the incursions of the Vikings continued. In 866CE a major raid was carried out on the Picts by 'the foreigners of Ireland and 'Scotland'. These were the Vikings who had settled in both countries, the north of Scotland and the Northern Isles having effectively been ceded to Viking control as early as 850CE. These 'foreigners' were effectively the first of the Gall-Gael, the hybrid society created by the mixture of the indigenous Q-Celtic speaking peoples and the incoming Germanic speaking Vikings. The *Annals of Ulster* for that year says they raided the whole of the lands of the Picts and 'took hostages from them' [Anderson 1990, 1 p.296]. From this distance it is impossible to say whether this means hostages were taken for specifically political reasons or that people were taken as slaves, which was common at the time. Whatever the reality it seems the Picts suffered a heavy defeat at the hands of the Vikings and Anderson suggests [*Ibid*] that the Vikings may well have been in Pictish lands for over two months. Two years after this the rampaging Vikings laid siege to and eventually took and destroyed Dumbarton, the capital of the Britons of Strathclyde and carried 'a great host' as captives, that is slaves, back to Ireland. This host of slaves is said in the Annals to have contained English, Britons and Picts [*Ibid*, pp.302–3].

In 872CE the then king of the Strathclyde Britons, Artgal, was slain 'by counsel of Constantine, Kenneth's son' [*Ibid*, p.304]. This would appear to be Constantine taking advantage of the ongoing troubled times to either settle an old account or to extend his own power in some way. By this period the land still under control of the Picts had diminished considerably with much of northern Scotland, the Northern Isles and the Hebrides being under Viking rule. While there are few early references to the Hebrides, particularly the outer isles, it is probably safe to assume the people there were in some way related to the Picts of mainland Scotland. The Vikings were not a united force and there were ongoing disputes among different sections of them rendering the politics of the period extremely complex. It is worth noting though that those who settled in Scotland and Ireland were prone to carrying on the travelling and raiding practices of their forefathers and it was from Ireland and the Hebrides that the eventual colonisation of Iceland took place in the 870s.

In 875CE there was another massive raid, this time by Danish Vikings and again the Picts suffered heavy losses. Two years later the raiders were back again and Constantine was killed leading the battle against them at a place called Inverdufath, which may well be Inverdovat in north-east Fife. In this battle the Picts suffered substantial losses as well as losing their leader and in a telling phrase from later Irish Annals 'the earth gave way under the men of Scotland' [*Ibid*, p.351]. Whatever stability we may imagine as a result of Constantine ruling for 15 or 16 years, after the confusion of the period immediately prior to his reign, must be offset by the obvious constant battles with the Vikings leading to his own eventual death in battle.

However another reference, though again not contemporary, has him being killed near a place called Black Cave [*Ibid*, p.354] and there is a Constantine's Cave on the south side of the Fife peninsula near Fife Ness about 27 miles south-east of Inverdovat. This cave has rough carvings of crosses and two indistinct animals and may be related to this or the later Constantine in the 10th century.

With Constantine's death the leadership fell to Aed, his brother. There is little information concerning his short reign though the *Annals of Ulster* put his death in 878CE, ominously telling us that he 'was slain by his own associates...' The later *Chronicle of the Kings of Scotland* is more specific, telling us that

> Aed, Kenneth's son, reigned for one year; and he was killed in the battle of Strathallan, by Giric, Dungal's son; and he was buried in Iona.
>
> [Anderson 1990, p.357]

It is clearly impossible to be sure what the motivation for this was but both sources agree that Aed was killed by his own people. Perhaps this was because he was not resisting the Vikings as much as was necessary but we should remember that dynastic squabbling and assassination are common to the supposed élite structures of many human societies throughout history. The location of this battle is quite specific, Strathallan, the valley of the Allan Water running northeast from modern Dunblane along the northern edge of the Ochil Hills, whose name is itself Pictish.

With Giric we come to the last of the Pictish kings. He was the son of Donald, Kenneth MacAlpin's brother who had ruled briefly and the assassination of Aed can be seen as primarily a family affair. As Woolf points out [2007, p.117f] the references to the period after Aed's death are from much later and are quite confusing. By 900 the new designation of Alba had come into being and there are no further references to the Picts. The contemporary Irish sources do not mention Giric and Aed is the last Pictish ruler they mention. In a later chronicle source Giric is said to have given 'liberties to the Scottish church, which had lain under the Pictish law' [Anderson 1990, p.368], which seems to mark some kind of clear break with the past, at least in terms of religion. After Giric's death in or around 889CE we hear no more of the Picts in any sources referring to the period.

CHAPTER ELEVEN

Then and now

THE PICTS WERE WRITTEN out of history – but they did not disappear physically. While disappearing from contemporary literary records they continued to have a role in the history of the Scottish people through the process we nowadays think of as folklore. From the border with England to the Shetland Islands stories of the Picts survived and a variety of ancient monuments were given the appellation of Pictish. The fact that such ancient monuments range from the prehistoric Pict's Knowe (nowadays called Piper's Knowe) at Ednam in the Borders to the medieval Picts' Dyke near Butterstone in Perth and Kinross, shows that in the imagination of the people as a whole, which is both where and how folklore survives, the Picts continued to be understood as the ancestor people of Scotland. They did not disappear. What disappeared was written references to them. Written references that do survive, generally through much later copies, come from a narrow section of society and mainly appear to reflect political changes happening at an élite level, as the tribal peoples of Pictish and Scottish origin combined to form the new political entity of Alba which in turn became Scotland. This new entity arising from the combination of the Picts and Scots reflected earlier times in that the political development was to a great extent brought about by external pressure, particularly from Scandinavian incomers. In this new polity the Dalriadan experience of greater political cohesion and centralisation, due to their particular geo-physical environment, was of considerable significance.

While our understanding of the period of the First Millennium comes to a considerable extent through extant texts in Latin and Gaelic, this tells us little about the Pictish language. What seems clear is that it probably never had a written form so is textually and thus historically invisible. When it ceased as a language of everyday communication is impossible to ascertain, but it certainly must have continued for a considerable period after the emergence of the new united society. Sadly we do not have any of the Picts' own words to help us better understand them. Batey tells us:

The recognition of the Picts as a 'people' serves more to confuse than illuminate. Scholars find it difficult to agree because of the lack of corroborative evidence, but they are probably the descendants of native Bronze Age incomers... and thus of the broch dwellers themselves. At any rate we do not have to see them as newcomers to Scotland, but rather as a development of what has gone before. They seem not to have been a single people, but probably a confederation of tribal units whose political motivations derived from a need to ally against common enemies.

[1993, p.115]

He is describing a situation that can also be seen to apply to the period when the Picts fade from history. Just as he sees the continuity from broch-builders – and earlier – to the Picts, so we should understand that the people referred to as Picts throughout most of the First Millennium simply evolved through time into modern Scots, intermingling with Dalriadans, Norse and incomers from elsewhere.

The political structures of the Picts had undergone many changes since the Romans attempted their subjugation and the same is of course true of their cousins, the Scots, with whom they now merged. The written references we do have were created by members of the Christian Church, an organisation philosophically and, to a great extent, politically rooted in a faraway place.

Given the domination of Christianity in the development of the Western intellectual tradition and the centrality of Classical studies to our understanding of the past it is little wonder that the Romans have been seen as so important. In the Scottish context however, this is unhelpful. Historical ideas change – the idea that major change can only come about through invasion is no longer acceptable and today we realise that the seas around Britain were not the hindrance to contact that they were thought to be. The idea that the Picts 'must' have come from elsewhere is no longer a cornerstone of our attempts to understand them. And if Dalriada was occupied by people who were as indigenous as the Pictish tribes – as would appear to be the case – we have the basis for understanding Scotland's history as being a continuum that has the Picts and the Scots as descendants of the earlier indigenous peoples and the ancestors of those who came after them. By this model of understanding the merging of the two tribal peoples in the 10th century can be seen as a natural

development, and though driven by external pressures, based on essentially shared experiences and understanding. Both peoples, or tribal groupings, were severely affected by the expansionist policies of Northumbria
and later by the Viking raids. While the Picts of the first century are said
to have come together to battle the Romans at Mons Graupius out of
military necessity, by the ninth century political and religious developments ensured that they would be better off working together rather
than maintaining separate identities or polities.

For most people life would probably not have altered much on a daily
basis as the new polity emerged. The men were farmers and warriors
before, they were farmers and warriors afterwards, the women were
mothers and farmers. In the new political situation the need to be ready
to resist external aggression was ever present, and this was a situation
that effectively continued to be a fundamental aspect of Scottish history
till the dawn of the 18th century. At the heart of the society that grew
from Alba into Scotland and expanded to include the lands south of the
Forth–Clyde line, were the tribal peoples who had been Picts and Scots
who became known simply as Scots. And even after Scotland was absor-
bed into English-dominated Britain, the descendants of those earlier tribes
were still ready to come forth from their Highland fastnesses to threaten
the very existence of the burgeoning British Empire. The cattle-raiding
Highland caterans that provided much of the Jacobite army as late as
1745 were in many ways the direct descendants of the Picts who had
fought off the Romans.

The similarities between Scottish and Pictish society and the inter-
relationships hinted at in the King Lists suggest that too much emphasis
has been laid on the differences between them. This may well have
resulted from the focus not being on Pictish society as a whole but on
their leaders, the fascination with élite behaviour obscuring rather than
illuminating our understanding. What we see in later years when Scotland
extended south of the Forth–Clyde line and incorporated what were once
the lands of the Gododdin and the Strathclyde Britons can be seen almost
as a return to the situation at the time of the Roman incursions, though
by now tribal society has evolved and there is a clear centralised political
superstructure. We may now be called Scots but the truth of the matter
is that a great many of us are indeed descended from the Picts and the
history of the Picts is the early history of the Scottish people.

The fact is that the Picts were tribal when the Romans arrived and parts of their territory were still effectively tribal as late as the 18th century. If it is correct that many settlements outside the Highland areas continued to be occupied throughout the Pictish period till the time of the Agricultural Revolution, as suggested by Professor Devine in his Edinburgh Lecture 2008, such economic continuity suggests other, socio-political continuities too. The Picts may have disappeared from the pages of written history by the close of the ninth century, but the people the name represents did not disappear, and their descendants continued to inhabit the same landscape.

Throughout much of the medieval period the Church in Scotland was heavily influenced from Ireland and the survival of Gaelic texts combined with the belief that Dalriada was an Irish colony, tended to downplay the importance of the Picts. The Reformation in Scotland saw a widespread destruction of manuscripts and artefacts that the fanatical Protestant mobs saw as being Papist. This, combined with the devastating effects of the disappearance of virtually all our indigenous early records, has meant that the Picts have ended up being portrayed as mysterious, unknowable and thus basically irrelevant to the needs of modern society. The fortunate survival of the Pictish symbol stones has left us with a truly great corpus of sculpture that has all too often tended to tantalise rather than inform. In recent years interest in the Picts has grown considerably and it is to be hoped that clearer understanding of our Pictish past will in time lead to a greater capacity to interpret the symbol stones, which will in turn help to clarify our ideas regarding the Picts even more. In this work I hope I have gone some way towards showing that though there is much, much more to be learned about our Pictish past, there is a picture that can be seen, a story that can be told.

While it is unlikely that we will ever come across previously unknown written sources for Scotland in the First Millennium – though not impossible – the increasing sophistication of archaeological technology may well allow us further insights to the Picts. This combined with developments in dating and DNA technologies will hopefully also give opportunities for increased understanding. It is to be hoped that new interpretations of the symbols themselves may provide a platform for positing future questions particularly concerning the pre-Christian period. After all archaeologists need to have some idea of what they are looking for when they investigate sites and greater insight into what may have been the belief structure of the indigenous people could be of considerable assistance in developing our understanding of the Picts, and how they relate to both those who were here before them, and those who came after.

However it seems clear just who the Picts were. They were the indigenous tribal peoples of the northern half of the British Isles when this part of the world first came into written history. Before the arrival of the Romans it is likely that Pictish society was part of a continuum of tribal pastoral peoples who occupied most of Britain and were closely related to such northern English tribes as the Brigantes and to the peoples in Ireland. They were also part of a continuum of society that suggests their own ancestors were the earlier Megalith-building peoples of these islands. While the Romans seem to have used the term Pict as a generic term referring to all of the tribal peoples north of Hadrian's Wall, using their own version of an extant local name, by the time Christianity arrived for good in the sixth century, the Picts can be seen as the tribal peoples north of the Forth–Clyde line. Over the ensuing centuries, while the population mainly continued to live in an established pattern – in time their small communities growing into the Lowland fermtouns and the Highland clachans – the combined influence of external military and political pressures and of the highly structured and literate Christian Church led to a centralised politico-military structure that laid the basis for what would in time become the Kingdom of the Scots. This development was likely to have been greatly influenced by the original Scots of Argyll whose initial westward vision – to the Isles and Ireland – became part of the unifying process that saw the Pictish and Scottish tribes finally cementing their long mutual involvement into the kingdom of Alba in the 10th century.

The Picts called themselves something like Pechts, the people of Scotland were still using the term into the modern era and they meant our ancestors. For me that is who they are.

Bibliography

URL references are to sources on the Worldwide Web. The organisations hosting these resources have been added in case of any future change in access.

Allen, R. and Anderson, J.; *The Early Christian Monuments of Scotland*; Pinkfoot Press; Balgavies, Forfar; 1993 (reprint)

Ammianus Marcellinus; trans Rolfe, J.C.; 3 vols; Harvard University Press; Cambridge, Mass; 1940

Anderson, Alan Orr; *Early Sources of Scottish History*: AD 500–1286, 2 Vols; Oliver and Boyd; Edinburgh; 1922

Anderson, M.; *Kings and Kingship in Early Scotland*; Scottish Academic Press; Edinburgh; 1973

Adomnan; *Life of Columba*; http://www.fordham.edu/halsall/basis/columba-e. html Fordham University, The Jesuit University of New York

Annals of Ulster; http://www.ucc.ie/celt/published/T100001A/index.html; CELT: Corpus of Electronic Texts, The Free Digital Humanities Resource for Irish history, literature and politics

Barclay, G.J.; *Proceedings of the Society of the Antiquaries of Scotland*; Vol 76; Number 293; pp.777–83, 2002

Bede; trans Sherley-Price, L; *A History of the English Church and People*; Penguin; London; 1955

Bower, Walter; Watt, D.E.R. [Ed]; *Scotichronicon*; Aberdeen University Press; Aberdeen; 1989

Broun, D.; 'Pictish Kings 761–836: integration with Dal Riata or separate development?' in Foster, S [Ed]; *The St Andrews Sarcophagus*; Historic Scotland; Edinburgh; 1998

Broun D.; *Scottish Independence and the Idea of Britain from the Picts to Alexander III*; Edinburgh University Press; 2007

Broun, D.; 'The genealogical 'tractates' associated with *Míniugud senchusa fher nAlban* and the creation of the Dál Riata ancestry of kings of Alba'; *Northern Scotland* Vol 20; 1–29; 2008

Burt, E.; Simmons, A. [Ed]; *Burt's Letters from the North of Scotland*; Birlinn; Edinburgh; 1998

Caesar, J.; *The Gallic War*; http://www.gutenberg.org/files/10657/10657. txt; Project Gutenberg, the first producer of free electronic books

Calder C.S.T.; 'Report on the Discovery of Numerous Stone Age House-Sites in Shetland'; *Proceedings of the Society of Antiquaries of Scotland*; Edinburgh; pp.340–97; 1955–6

Campbell, E.; 'Were the Scots Irish?'; *Antiquity* Vol 75 No 288; pp285–92; 2001

Caradoc of Llangafran, *Life of Gildas*; http://www.fordham.edu/halsall/basis/1150-*Caradoc-LifeofGildas.html*; Internet Medieval Sourcebook, Fordham University, The Jesuit University of New York

Cessford, C.; 'A Lost Pictish Poem?'; *Scottish Literary Journal* Vol 23; pp.7–15; Nov 1996

Clancy, T.O.; 'The real St Ninian'; *Innes Review* 52; 2001

Clancy, T.O.; 'Philosopher-King: Nechtan Mac Der-Ilei'; *Scottish Historical Review*; pp125–48; 2004

Claudian; trans Platnauer, M.; 2 vols; Heinemann; London; 1922

Cunliffe, B.; *Facing the Ocean*; Oxford University Press; Oxford; 2001

Dio Cassius; trans Cary, E; *Dio's Roman History*, Heinemann; London; 1927

Edrich, M. Gianotta, K.M. and Hanson W.; 'Traprain Law: native and Roman on the northern frontier'; *Proceedings of the Society of Antiquaries of Scotland*; Edinburgh; Vol 130; pp.451–6; 2000

Eichholz, D.E.; 'Constantius Chlorus' Invasion of Britain'; *Journal of Roman Studies* 43; pp.41–6; 1953

Forsyth, K.; *Language in Pictland*; de Keltische Draak; Utrecht; 1997

Foster, S. [Ed]; *The St Andrews Sarcophagus*; Historic Scotland; Edinburgh; 1998

Fraser, J.; *From Caledonia to Pictland: Scotland to 795*; Edinburgh University Press; 2009

Frere, S.; *Britannia; A History of Roman Britain*; Routledge & Kegan Paul; London; 1987

Gildas; Winterbottom, M. [Ed]; Phillimore; London; 1978

Ginzburg, C.; *Ecstasies*; Hutchinson Radius; London; 1990

Gourlay, R.; 'Before the Vikings: The pre-Norse background in Caithness'; in Batey, C.E., Jesch, J., Morris, C. [Eds]; *The Viking Age in Caithness, Orkney and the North Atlantic*; Edinburgh University Press; Edinburgh; 1993

Gray, K.A.; 'A new look at the Pictish King List'; *Pictish Arts Society Journal 10*; PAS; Edinburgh; pp.7–13; 1996

Hedeager, L.; trans Hines, J.; *Iron Age Socieies: From Tribe to State in Northern Europe 500BC to AD 700*; Blackwell; London; 1992

Henderson, I.; *The Picts*; Thames & Hudson; London; 1967

Herodian; trans Whittaker, C.R.; Heinemann; Harvard University Press; Cambridge, Mass; 1949

James, S.; *The Atlantic Celts, Ancient People or Modern Invention?*; British Museum Press; London; 1999

Lyle, E.; 'The Importance of the Prehistory of Indo-European Structures for Indo-European Studies'; *Journal of Indo-European Studies* 34, Nos 1&2; pp.99–110; 2006

McHardy, S.A.; *School of the Moon*; Birlinn; Edinburgh; 2004

McHardy, S.A.; *The Quest for Arthur*; Luath Press; Edinburgh; 2001

McHardy, S.A.; *The Quest for the Nine Maidens*; Luath Press; Edinburgh; 2003

McHardy, S.A.; 'What's in a Name?'; *Pictish Arts Society Journal* 9; pp.14–16; 1992

McHardy, S.A.; 'The Wee Dark Fowk o Scotland'; in Henry, David; *The Worm, the Germ and the Thorn; Pictish and related studies presented to Isabel Henderson*; Pinkfoot Press; Balgavies, Angus; 1997

McHardy, S.A.; *On the Trail of Scotland's Myths and Legends*; Luath Press; Edinburgh; 2005

McHardy, S.A.; On the Trail of the Holy Grail; Luath Press; Edinburgh; 2006

Maclean, D.; 'The Northumbrian Perspective'; in Foster, S. [Ed]; *The St Andrews Sarcophagus*; Historic Scotland; Edinburgh; 1998

McNeill, F.M.; *The Silver Bough*; 4 vols; William MacLellan; Glasgow; 1957, I; 1959, II; 1961, III; 1968, IV

Miller, M.; 'The disputed historical horizon of the Pictish king-lists'; *Scottish Historical Review 58*; pp.1–105; 1979

Merlsford; http://canmore.rcahms.gov.uk/en/site/27776/details/merlsford Royal Commission on Ancient and Historical Monuments

Millar, F.; *Dio Cassius*; Clarendon Press; Oxford; 1964

Moffat, B.; *A Marvellous Plant*; Folio No 1 National Library of Scotland; 2000

Nennius; *Historia Brittonum*; http://www.fordham.edu/halsall/basis/nennius-full.html; Fordham University, The Jesuit University of New York

Ninian, St; *Ninian, Enlightener of the Picts*; http://www.voskrese.info/spl/Xninian-whith.html; Saint Pachomius Library

Nixon, C.E.V.; *In Praise of Roman Emperors*; University of California Press; Berkeley; 1994

Oram, R.D.; *Scottish Prehistory*; Birlinn; Edinburgh; 1997

Phillpotts, Bertha; *Kindred and Clan*; Cambridge University Press; Cambridge; 1913

Pittock, M.; *Jacobitism*; Palgrave Macmillan; London; 1998

Rees, A. & Rees, B.; *Celtic Heritage*; Thames and Hudson; London; 1990

Rivet, A.L.F. & Smith, C.; *The Place-Names of Roman Britain*; Batsford Ltd; London; 1979

Patrick, St; *Letter to Coroticus*; http://www.yale.edu/glc/archive/1166.htm; Yale University

Salway, P.; *Roman Britain*; Clarendon Press; London; 1981

Sawyer, P.; *Kings and Vikings*; Methuen; London; 1982

Scott, W.; *Manners, Customs and History of the Highlanders of Scotland*; Morison; Glasgow; 1893

Simpson, W.D.; 'Corgarff Castle'; *Proceedings of the Society of Antiquaries of Scotland* Vol LXI; pp.48–111; Edinburgh; 1926

Smyth, A.P.; *Warlords and Holy Men*; Edward Arnold; London; 1984

Solinus; Golding, A. [Ed]; *The Excellent and Pleasant Worke: Collectanea Rerum Memorabilium of Caius Julius Solinus*; New York; 1999 [reprint]

Swan, V.G.; 'The Twentieth Legion and the history of the Antonine Wall reconsidered'; in *Proceedings of the Society of Antiquaries of Scotland* Vol 129; pp.399–481; 1999

Sykes, B.; *Blood of the Isles*; Bantam; London; 2006

Valesianus; *The Anonymous Valesianus*; http://penelope.uchicago.edu/Thayer/E/Roman/Texts/Excerpta_Valesiana/home.htm; University of Chicago

Watson, W.J.; *The Celtic Place Names of Scotland*; Birlinn; Edinburgh; 1994 [reprint]

Watson, W.J.; 'The Picts; their original position in Scotland'; from Transactions of the Gaelic Society of Inverness Vol xxx; 1925 Papers

Wainwright, F.T. [Ed]; *The Problem of the Picts*; Melven Press; Perth; 1980

Woolf A.; 'Dun Nechtain, Fortriu and the Geography of the Picts'; *Scottish Historical Review* LXXX; Vol 2 No 220; pp.182–201; 2006

Woolf, A.; *From Pictland to Alba 789–1070*; Edinburgh University; 2007

Woolliscroft, D.J.; http://www.theromangaskproject.org.uk/Pages/Introduction/Gask_signalling.html; The Roman Gask Project

Young, J.D.; *The Very Bastards of Creation*; Clydeside Press; Glasgow; 1996

Zimmerman, D.; *The Jacobite Movement in Scotland and in Exile 1746–1759*; Palgrave Macmillan; Basingstoke; 2003

Time Line

55 BCE	Romans land in southern Britain
43 CE	Claudius invades Britain
70–80	Gask ridge forts built
81	Battle of Mons Graupius; Calgacus leads Caledonian Confederation
85	Fort at Inchtuthil abandoned
108	Roman positions north of Tyne–Solway destroyed
122–36	Building of Hadrian's Wall
143–8	Building of Antonine Wall
164	Antonine Wall abandoned
180-5	Hadrian's Wall overrun
208	Re-manning of forts on Hadrian's Wall by Septimus Severus
211	Death of Severus, Roman withdrawal to Hadrian's Wall
306	Constantine proclaimed Roman emperor at York. Frontier consolidated
367	Barbarian Conspiracy overruns Hadrian's Wall
387	Roman Garrisons leave frontier
400	Germanic-speaking mercenaries consolidate Northumbria
407	Last Romans leave Britain
405–500	Earliest Christian cemeteries Whithorn and Kirkmadrine in use
500	Floruit of Ninian. Fergus mac Erc dies
525–550	Bernicia formed by Angles centred on Bamburgh
563	Columba exiled to lands in Alba
570	Floruit of Ryderch Hen of Strathclyde
570–600	Floruit of Kentigern
574	Columba ordains Aedan Mac Gabhran, king of Dalriada
585	Death of Bridei mac Maelchon
590	Urien of Rheged killed at siege of Lindisfarne
593–617	Northumbrian expansion under Ethelfrith
c.600	Gododdin raid
603	Aedan mac Gabhran beaten at Degastan by Ethelfrith
c.608	Aedan dies
617	Martyrdom of St Donnan on Eigg
617–33	Edwin becomes king of Northumbria. Oswald and Oswiu exiled amongst Picts and Scots
629–42	Domnall Brecc king of Scots
634–41	Oswald king of Northumbria

634–51	Bishop Aidan controls Northumbrian church
638	Northumbrian assault on Edinburgh
641–70	Oswiu king of Bernicia and from 655 of Northumbria
653–57	Talorcan son of Eanfrith king of Picts
660–80	Northumbrian conquest of Rheged
664	Synod of Whitby
670–85	Ecgfrith king of Northumbria
672	Drest deposed and Picts massacred by Ecgfrith
679	Adomnan Abbot of Iona
681	Anglian bishopric at Abercorn
685	Battle of Dunnichen
685–705	Aldfrith king of Northumbria
688–92	*Life of Columba* written
c.700	Re-establishment of Eigg
70d	Adomnan dies
706–24	Nechtan mac Derile king of Picts
711	Picts slaughtered by Saxons in plain of Manaw
717	Nechtan expels Columban clergy
729–61	Oengus I king of Picts
750	Eadbeht of Northumbria conquers Kyle
750–2	Teudubr, son of Bili, king of Strathclyde rules Picts
780–6	*Book of Kells* begun on Iona
793	Viking raid on Lindisfarne
795	Vikings lay waste Skye and Iona
802	Vikings attack Iona again
807–14	New church at Kells for Iona *familia*
811–20	Constantine son of Fergus, king of Dalriada and Picts
820–34	Oengus II, son of Fergus king of Dalriada and Picts
839	Major Viking victory over Picts
840	Kenneth MacAlpin king of DalRiata
c.847	Kenneth king of Scots and Picts
850–70	Viking domination of the west
858–62	Donald I king of Picts and Scots. Laws of Dalriada read at Forteviot
862	Constantine king of Picts and Scots
866–7	Danes conquer Northumbria
866–9	Olaf the White attacks the Picts
870–90	Migration of Scottish Vikings to Iceland
875	Halfdan attacks Picts and Britons of Strathclyde
877	Aed king of Picts and Scots
878–	Giric, last king of Picts
900	Scots annex Strathclyde

Index

Luath Press Limited

committed to publishing well written books worth reading

LUATH PRESS takes its name from Robert Burns, whose little collie Luath (*Gael.*, swift or nimble) tripped up Jean Armour at a wedding and gave him the chance to speak to the woman who was to be his wife and the abiding love of his life. Burns called one of 'The Twa Dogs' Luath after Cuchullin's hunting dog in Ossian's *Fingal*. Luath Press was established in 1981 in the heart of Burns country, and now resides a few steps up the road from Burns' first lodgings on Edinburgh's Royal Mile.

Luath offers you distinctive writing with a hint of unexpected pleasures.

Most bookshops in the UK, the US, Canada, Australia, New Zealand and parts of Europe either carry our books in stock or can order them for you. To order direct from us, please send a £sterling cheque, postal order, international money order or your credit card details (number, address of cardholder and expiry date) to us at the address below. Please add post and packing as follows: UK – £1.00 per delivery address; overseas surface mail – £2.50 per delivery address; overseas airmail – £3.50 for the first book to each delivery address, plus £1.00 for each additional book by airmail to the same address. If your order is a gift, we will happily enclose your card or message at no extra charge.

Luath Press Limited
543/2 Castlehill
The Royal Mile
Edinburgh EH1 2ND
Scotland
Telephone: 0131 225 4326 (24 hours)
Fax: 0131 225 4324
email: sales@luath.co.uk
Website: www.luath.co.uk